Seven Skills of Media Literacy

W. James Potter
University of California, Santa Barbara

Los Angeles | London | New Delhi
Singapore | Washington DC | Melbourne

FOR INFORMATION:

SAGE Publications, Inc.
2455 Teller Road
Thousand Oaks, California 91320
E-mail: order@sagepub.com

SAGE Publications Ltd.
1 Oliver's Yard
55 City Road
London, EC1Y 1SP
United Kingdom

SAGE Publications India Pvt. Ltd.
B 1/I 1 Mohan Cooperative Industrial Area
Mathura Road, New Delhi 110 044
India

SAGE Publications Asia-Pacific Pte. Ltd.
18 Cross Street #10-10/11/12
China Square Central
Singapore 048423

Printed in the United States of America

ISBN: 9781544378565

This book is printed on acid-free paper.

Acquisitions Editor: Lily Norton
Editorial Assistant: Sarah Wilson
Production Editor: Bennie Clark Allen
Copy Editor: Christina West
Typesetter: Hurix Digital
Proofreader: Eleni Maria Georgiou
Cover Designer: Candice Harman
Marketing Manager: Staci Wittek

SUSTAINABLE FORESTRY INITIATIVE
Certified Sourcing
www.sfiprogram.org
SFI-01075

19 20 21 22 23 10 9 8 7 6 5 4 3 2 1

Seven Skills
of Media Literacy

Sara Miller McCune founded SAGE Publishing in 1965 to support the dissemination of usable knowledge and educate a global community. SAGE publishes more than 1000 journals and over 800 new books each year, spanning a wide range of subject areas. Our growing selection of library products includes archives, data, case studies and video. SAGE remains majority owned by our founder and after her lifetime will become owned by a charitable trust that secures the company's continued independence.

Los Angeles | London | New Delhi | Singapore | Washington DC | Melbourne

Contents

3 Analyzing: Digging Into the Meaning and Structure of Media Messages 37

4 Evaluating: Making Judgments About the Value of Media Messages 57

7

Deducing: Reasoning with Logic from General Principles

115

8

Synthesizing: Assembling Novel Configurations

129

Preface

A great deal has been written about the topic of media literacy. If you do a Google search on this topic, you will get almost 5 million hits. If you narrow the search down to only scholarly publications, a search of Google Scholar will result in almost 2 million hits. If you start reading these publications, you will notice they are written by people from every country in the world and every background, including social scientists, consumer activists, elected officials, government employees, parents, and educators from all levels.

There are three main themes that pervade this large media literacy literature. First, almost all authors claim that in our information-saturated culture, media influence is pervasive and continuous. Second, authors argue that the best chance people have of controlling that media influence on themselves is to increase their levels of media literacy. And third, authors maintain that an essential part of media literacy is the development of skills that can be used to process meaning from media messages more accurately and deeply, thereby helping people use the media for their own purposes and protect themselves from the risks of experiencing negative effects.

While this literature is rich in breadth with many ideas, it lacks much depth of detail. This is especially the case when authors write about skills. Few authors who argue for the importance of skills articulate what those skills are. Although there is frequent mention of something referred to as "critical thinking," hardly anyone defines what this is, how to train people on this skill, or how to measure it.

As I have been reading this literature over the past several decades, it has become clear to me that when authors use the general term "media literacy skills" to argue for the development of higher levels of media literacy, they are envisioning tasks that could be accomplished more effectively and efficiently with the generic skills that people already have. Therefore, I have been arguing that the development of each person's level of media literacy does not require the learning of new, exotic skills; instead, it requires that we better understand the skills we already have and that we be provided with enough detail to guide our improvement. This is the cutting edge of this literature; that is, while scholars continually call for improvement of media literacy skills, there are currently no writings anywhere in this vast literature that provide enough detail to serve as a useful set of detailed guidelines to help people improve the essential skills they need when interacting with media messages. This book provides such a set of guidelines by focusing attention on what I have identified as the seven skills of media literacy: analyzing, evaluating, grouping, inducing, deducing, synthesizing, and abstracting.

With each of these skills that we use in our everyday lives, there is a wide range of performance potential. We can always improve. And those improvements can pay huge dividends by increasing our ability to use media messages to satisfy our own needs much better, while avoiding the potential risks of being manipulated by the media to serve only their needs and thereby increase our risk of experiencing negative media effects.

My purpose in this book is to show you what these seven skills are in detail and to provide you with guidelines to help you increase your abilities in using each of these skills. My approach in fulfilling this purpose is more practical than theoretical. That is, I present easy-to-follow guidelines illustrated with everyday examples. Then I offer many exercises to help you practice using these guidelines.

The core of this book is seven chapters, one for each of the seven skills. In these chapters (Chapter 3 through Chapter 9), I will clarify what each of these skills is. Each of these chapters presents a clear procedure—called an algorithm—for using the skill featured in that chapter. In presenting these algorithms, I have tried to make them appear simple in order to make them as clear and as useful as possible. However, in doing so, it was not possible to present a set of steps that could cover all usages of a particular skill; the range of challenges that we encounter when we interact with media messages is just too varied. So to help readers use these skills successfully when the algorithms alone do not provide enough guidance, I have also included heuristics. These heuristics are "rules of thumb" that can help you understand how to increase your ability to use the skills over and above the guidance presented in the list of steps presented in the algorithms. Also, each chapter has a section that shows you how to avoid traps when using these skills.

As a foundation for the seven skills chapters, I present two initial chapters that demonstrate why skills development is so important to media literacy (Chapter 1) and why these particular seven skills are the essential core to your personal improvement (Chapter 2). The book concludes with Chapter 10, which presents a big-picture perspective about how these skills work together in meeting the challenges of media literacy.

The core resources in this book are the guidelines (algorithms, heuristics, and avoiding traps) and the exercises. Your improvement is keyed to how well you understand the guidelines and how much you practice applying those guidelines—first in the book's exercises, then second in your everyday lives as you encounter media messages. As you work through these exercises, you will assess your initial levels of these skills and then you will monitor how well you are improving. If your purpose in using this book is to help other people develop their skills of media literacy, then these guidelines will be useful in constructing your instructional lessons, and the exercises will help you monitor the progress of those people you are trying to help. And if your purpose is to conduct empirical studies to help contribute to our knowledge about media literacy, this book will serve as a valuable guide for designing interventions to teach these skills as well as designing measures to assess changes in skills exhibited by your research participants.

Skills in the Context of Media Literacy

Because the focus of this book is to help you develop the key skills of media literacy, it is important to start with some context so you can understand why these skills are essential to developing higher levels of media literacy. In this chapter, I will first highlight the main ideas that people use when talking about this broad idea we label as "media literacy." Then I will present some key ideas about the nature of skills. This information will provide you with a good foundation to understand why the seven skills highlighted in this book are so essential to media literacy.

I. What Is Media Literacy?

Many people evoke the term *media literacy* as a way of dealing with a wide range of problems they perceive as being generated by the mass media. These people include politicians, consumer activists, parents, educators, and academics. As you might imagine, there is a wide variety of meanings circulating about this term. Setting aside all the nuances of different meanings, we can see that there is a core set of ideas that almost everyone who uses the term seems to share. It is important that you understand what these ideas are so that you can appreciate why increasing your own levels of media literacy can significantly help you in your everyday life.

Shared Ideas

In the Preface, I pointed out three ideas that pervade the media literacy literature. Now, I will narrow our focus down to the ideas of skills and point out four ideas about how authors regard the nature of skills as tools of media literacy. These four ideas are as follows:

1. Media literacy skills should be regarded broadly so their utility is not limited to any one medium or any one type of message;

2. The purpose of skills of media literacy is twofold; that is, using these skills can do more than simply protect people from unwanted effects—these skills can also empower people to use the media more strategically to satisfy their individual needs;

3. These skills are best regarded along a continuum where we all have some level of ability with them; and

4. The skills of media literacy are not static and therefore they can be developed with the right kind of training.

Let's examine each of these four ideas in more detail.

Broad Perspective on Media

All definitions of media literacy are broad in the sense that they refer to skills that can be used to address challenges across all kinds of media and messages. They are not limited to one medium. Initially, the term *literacy* referred to a person's ability to read the written word—that is, translate arbitrary symbols of letters, words, and sentences into various levels of meaning. However, with the advent of technologies to convey messages visually in addition to print, the idea of literacy was expanded to include terms like *visual literacy* (the ability to translate flat two-dimensional images into real-world three-dimensional understandings), *story literacy* (the ability to follow narratives in film and video that use truncated action, limited frames, editing, sound, and other storytelling conventions), and *computer literacy* (the ability to record one's own messages, to send them to others electronically, to search for messages, and to process meaning from electronic screens). Most people who use the term *media literacy* refer to people's ability to perceive meaning from any medium or type of message.

Purpose of Protecting and Empowering

Early writing about media literacy focused on using skills exclusively to protect people from unwanted negative effects from the media. This meaning grew from the public's generalized fear that as each new medium was introduced (especially film, radio, and television), the population was being exposed to risks of negative effects from political propaganda, violence, and sexual portrayals. It was believed that the mass media were powerful influencers and that people needed to be protected from this constant, pervasive influence. Therefore, the initial purpose of media literacy was to help people avoid, or at least reduce, these risks of experiencing negative effects.

Now most authors who write about media literacy also argue that skills can be used in a proactively positive manner by empowering people to use the media to satisfy their own needs better than they could if their skills were weak. These authors do not reject the claim that the media often exert negative effects; instead, these authors also include the belief that the media exert many positive effects and that when media literacy is conceptualized as empowerment, its purpose is to help people increase the probability of experiencing positive effects while decreasing the probability of experiencing negative effects. Thus, media literacy is less about criticizing the media and more about analyzing potential media effects to identify the good as well as the bad. This expanded vision for media literacy makes it even more important for people to understand the skills they will need to achieve greater empowerment.

To illustrate this distinction between protection and empowerment, consider the way many people criticize the growth of social media. For example, there are critics who complain that the newer forms of technology have harmed people's ability to write well, because texting, instant messaging, and tweeting have pushed aside letter writing and longer forms of communication. An illustration of this belief is John Sutherland, an English professor at the University College of London, who has argued that texting has reduced language into a "bleak, bald, sad shorthand," that Facebook reinforces narcissistic drivel, and that PowerPoint presentations have taken the place of well-reasoned essays (quoted in Thompson, 2009). He says that today's technologies of communication that encourage or even require shorter messages, like Twitter, have shortened people's attention spans and therefore have limited their ability to think in longer arcs, which is required for constructing well-reasoned essays. In contrast, other people regard these newer formats for communication more positively. For example, Andrea Lunsford, a professor emerita of writing and rhetoric at Stanford University, argues that the newer information technologies have actually increased literacy. She says "I think we're in the midst of a literacy revolution the likes of which we haven't seen since Greek civilization" (quoted in Thompson, 2009). In addition, she argues that these new technologies of communication are not killing our ability to write well but instead are pushing it in new directions of being more personal, creative, and concise. She reached this conclusion after systematically analyzing more than 14,000 student writing samples over a 5-year period. She explains that young people today are adept at understanding the needs of their audiences and writing messages especially crafted to appeal to them. For today's youth, writing is about discovering themselves, organizing their thoughts concisely, managing impressions, and persuading their readers.

It is faulty to regard the media's influence on our skill set as being either all good or all bad. The challenge of developing higher levels of media literacy requires that we all improve certain skills so that we can more effectively tell the difference between potentially negative and potentially positive effects in our exposures to media messages.

Belief in a Continuum, Not a Category

While most authors regard media literacy skills as existing along a continuum, there are still some authors who seem to indicate that skills are categorical; that is, either a person has a skill or does not. This is a subtle but important distinction because if we regard skills as being categorical, then it gives people a false sense of preparedness when they believe they have any of these skills. Instead, people need to regard media literacy skills as existing along a wide continuum where there is always room for improvement.

We all occupy some position on the media literacy continuum. There is no point below which we could say that someone has no media literacy, and there is no point at the high end of the continuum where we can say that someone is fully media literate; there is always room for improvement.

Faith That Skills Can Be Developed

There is a widespread belief among media literacy scholars that people's levels of media literacy can be improved with the development of their skills. We all have a natural level of media literacy and that is good enough to enable us to do many things with the media. But there are also many things we cannot do with the media mainly because we have skills that are not developed well enough to allow us to examine many things that we simply take for granted. If we are to expand our understanding about the media so that we can see more opportunities for using the media to achieve our own goals while protecting ourselves from threats that we have been unable to perceive, then we need to increase the level of our essential media literacy skills.

Components

Although skills are essential to our development of greater levels of media literacy, they do not work alone. Skills are tools, so we need raw materials of information in order to build knowledge structures. Also, we need some drive energy to motivate our use of skills. Therefore, the key components of media literacy are skills, knowledge structures, and personal locus. All three components work together.

Skills

Many people write about media literacy as essentially being a skill. These definitions highlight the importance of people learning how to analyze media messages to see underlying meanings and to evaluate those messages along all kinds of dimensions such as credibility, realism, usefulness, and entertainment value.

What is the skill of media literacy? While many definers of this term offer no name for the skill they are arguing for, many do offer a name—typically "critical thinking." Although the term *critical thinking* sounds good, its use creates confusion because everyone seems to have a different meaning for it. Some people regard critical thinking as a willingness to criticize the media; other people define it as the need to examine issues in more depth; still others suggest a meaning of being more systematic and logical when interacting with the media; others imply that it means the ability to focus on the most important issues and ignore the rest; and the list goes on and on. In order to avoid this conglomeration of meanings, I avoid using this term; instead, I will try to be more clear by showing you how media literacy relies on seven specific skills. These are the skills of analysis, evaluation, grouping, induction, deduction, synthesis, and abstraction (see Table 1.1).

These skills are not exclusive to media literacy tasks; instead, we use these skills in all sorts of ways in our everyday lives. We all have some ability with each of these skills, so the media literacy challenge is *not to acquire*

TABLE 1.1	The Seven Skills of Media Literacy
Analyzing	The breaking down of a message into meaningful elements
Evaluating	The making of judgments about the value of elements; the judgment is made by comparing the element to some standard
Grouping	The determining of which elements are alike in some way and which elements are different in some way
Inducing	The inferring of general patterns from the observation of particulars; generalizing those patterns to larger aggregates; and the continual testing of those patterns
Deducing	Using general principles to explain particulars in a process of logical reasoning
Synthesizing	The assembling of elements into a novel structure to solve some problem or complete some partially specified task
Abstracting	The assembling of elements into a brief, clear, and accurate description of a message

these skills; rather our challenge is *to get better* at using each of these skills in our encounters with media messages.

Knowledge Structures

Another often-mentioned component in definitions of media literature is **information**, or the term I prefer—**knowledge structures**. In everyday language, the terms *information* and *knowledge* are often used as synonyms, but in this book, they have meanings very different from one another (see Table 1.2). Information is piecemeal and transitory, whereas knowledge is structured, organized, and of more enduring significance. Information resides in the messages, whereas knowledge resides in a person's mind. Information gives something to the person to interpret, whereas knowledge reflects that which has already been interpreted by the person. Information is composed of facts. Facts by themselves are not knowledge any more than a pile of lumber is a house. Knowledge requires structure to provide context and reveal meaning. Think of messages as the raw materials and think of skills as the tools you use to build your knowledge structures.

Knowledge structures are sets of organized information in your memory that help you see patterns that organize your world. We use these patterns as maps to tell us where to get more information and also where to go to retrieve information we have previously encoded into our knowledge structures. To help visualize this, think about your bedroom. Are your books, papers, clothes, food wrappers, and everything else randomly scattered all over your bed, desk, closet, and drawers? If so, is it difficult for you to find things?

TABLE 1.2   Contrasting Information with Knowledge

Information	Knowledge
Piecemeal	Structured and organized
Transitory	Enduring
Resides in messages	Resides in a person's mind
Raw material	Constructed from raw material
Value lies in accuracy	Value lies in context and meaning
Focused on individual facts	Focused on meaning arising from connections

Information is the essential ingredient in knowledge structures. But not all information is equally useful in the building of a knowledge structure. Some information is rather superficial. If all a person has is the recognition of surface information such as lyrics to television show theme songs, names of characters and actors, settings for shows, and the like, he or she is operating with a low level of media literacy, because this type of information addresses only the question of "what?" The more useful information comes in the form of the answers to the questions of "how?" and "why?" But remember that you first need to know something about the *what* before you can delve deeper into the *how* and *why*.

While I'm on the topic of distinguishing information from knowledge, I also need to define a few terms related to the idea of information: **message**, **factual information**, and **social information**. Messages are those instruments that deliver information to us. Information is the content of those messages. Messages can be delivered in many different media—computers, smartphones, television, radio, CDs, video games, books, newspapers, magazines, websites, conversations, lectures, concerts, street signs, products labels, and so on. They can be large (an entire Hollywood movie) or small (one utterance by one character in a movie).

Messages are composed of two kinds of information: factual and social. Facts are discrete bits of information, such as names (of people, places, characters, etc.), dates, titles, definitions of terms, formulas, lists, and the like. For example, when you watch the news and hear messages about terrorism, those messages are composed of facts, such as the following: *Donald Trump was elected to the office of President of the United States in the fall of 201* This statement contains bits of information that can be verified by comparir them to a truth standard.

Social information is composed of lessons that people infer fro observing social interactions. These lessons are inferred from the patterr of actions and consequences we observe. Thus, social information is cor posed of accepted beliefs that cannot be verified by authorities in the san way factual information can be. This is not to say that social information is less valuable or less real to people. The difference between factual information and social information lies in whether there is an objective basis that can be used to verify the accuracy of the information. With factual information, there is an objective truth standard; with social information, there is not.

Knowledge structures provide the context we use when trying to make sense of each new media message. The more knowledge structures we have, the more confident we can be in making sense of a wide range of messages. For example, you may have a very large, well-developed knowledge structure about a particular television series. You may know the names of all the characters in that TV show. You may know everything that has happened to those characters in all the episodes. You may even know the names and histories of the actors who play the characters. If you have all of this information well organized so that you can recall any of it at a moment's notice, you have a well-developed knowledge structure about that television series. Are you media literate? Within the small corner of the media world where that one TV show resides, you are. But if this were the only knowledge structure you had developed, you would have little understanding of the content produced by the other media. You would have difficulty understanding trends about who owns and controls the media, about how the media have developed over time, about why certain kinds of content are never seen while other types are continually repeated, and about what effects that content may be having on you. With many highly developed knowledge structures, you could understand the entire span of media issues and therefore be able to "see the big picture" about why the media are the way they are.

Knowledge structures must be constructed by us. The raw materials we use to construct them are bits of information. The tools we use to construct them are skills. Thus the more developed our skills are, the better are our tools to create and revise our knowledge structures.

Knowledge structures change as we deal with information. As we add new information, the knowledge structure becomes more elaborate and detailed. This makes it more useful to us. If the new information reveals that old information in our existing knowledge structure is out of date, we cut out the old and insert the new.

Personal Locus

Your **personal locus** is composed of goals and drives. The goals shape the information-processing tasks by determining what gets filtered in and what gets ignored. The more you are aware of your goals, the more you can direct the process of information seeking. And the stronger your drives for information are, the more effort you will expend to attain your goals. However, when your locus is weak (i.e., you are not aware of particular goals and your drive energy is low), you will default to media control where you allow the media to exercise a high degree of control over your media exposure patterns and over the way you process information from those exposures.

The more you know about your personal locus and the more you make conscious decisions to shape it, the more you can control the process of influence that the media are constantly exerting on you. The more you engage your personal locus, the more you will be increasing your media literacy.

Being media literate, however, does not require that your personal locus be fully engaged every minute of every day. That would be an unreasonable requirement, because no one can maintain a high degree of concentration all the time. Instead, the process of increasing media literacy requires you to activate your personal locus in bursts. During these periods of high concentration, you can analyze your **mental codes** to make sure that they are set up to achieve your own personal goals rather than the goals of media programmers or advertisers. To understand the nature of mental codes, think of an analogy where your body is a computer and your brain is the hard drive. When you are born, your brain already has some mental codes hard-wired into it—these are the codes that guide the functioning of your body's organs and perceptual systems. As you go through experiences in life, additional codes get written and stored in your brain. These additional codes are written by our parents, siblings, institutions, and the media. Most of these sources of programming codes are from agents who are trying to help us, but some of the code is programmed by agents who are more interested in helping themselves than helping us. For example, advertisers send out media messages in order to increase purchasing of their products and services; sometimes these messages really do help us but oftentimes, those messages do not help and can even hurt us. If our memory banks are dominated by programming that harms us while helping only the programmers' needs, then we are being exploited when those automatic codes are constantly running in the back of our minds. This is why it is important to periodically examine those automatic codes to make sure they are running to serve your own interests more so than the interests of other third parties.

These periods of examination will generate new insights about what is working well and where the glitches are. Then you can use those new insights to reprogram your mental code and fix the glitches by correcting faulty information, repairing uninformed opinions, and changing habits that are making you unhappy. Then once these alterations are made to your mental codes, you can return to automatic processing where your newly programmed codes will better help you achieve your goals for information and entertainment.

II. Nature of Skills

In this section, I will first draw a distinction between skills and competencies. Then I will describe what the core seven skills of media literacy are.

Skills Versus Competencies

In everyday language, the terms *skills* and *competencies* are used as synonyms. Yet it is important to make a distinction here. **Competencies** are the tools people have acquired to help them interact with the media and to access information in the messages. Competencies are learned early in life, then applied automatically. Competencies are categorical; that is, either people are able to do something or they are not able. For example, either people know how to recognize a word and match its meaning to a memorized meaning or they do not.

Skills, in contrast to competencies, are not categorical. Instead skills offer a wide continuum of performance. Skill development is what can make a large difference in a person moving from lower to higher levels of media literacy. People who have weak skills will not be able to do much with the information they encounter. For example, if their skill of analysis is weak, they will not be able to dig out the good information from media messages. If their skill of evaluation is weak, they will not be able to judge the quality or usefulness of information well, so they cannot tell which information is good and which is faulty. If their skills of grouping induction are weak, they will not be able to see patterns across different messages. If their skills of abstraction are weak, they will struggle to see the "big picture" in a message. And if their skills of deduction and synthesis are weak, they will have great difficulty incorporating new information into their knowledge structures. They will organize information poorly, thus creating weak and faulty knowledge structures. In the worst case, people with weak skills will try to avoid thinking about information altogether and become passive; as a consequence, the active information providers—such as advertisers, entertainers, and news workers—will increase their power as the constructors of people's knowledge structures and will take control over of how people see the world by altering their beliefs and by giving people faulty standards that they then use to create their attitudes.

Media literacy is not limited to competencies. Having competencies does not make one media literate, but lacking these competencies prevents one from being media literate because this deficiency prevents a person from accessing particular kinds of information. For example, people who do not have a basic reading competency cannot access printed material. This will greatly limit what they can build into their knowledge structures. This will also suppress the drive states in the personal locus; people who cannot read will have very low motivation to expose themselves to printed information.

Skills and competencies work together in a continual cyclical process. With certain information-processing tasks, some skills or competencies may be more important than others. For example, with the task of filtering, the skills of analysis and evaluation are most important. With the task of meaning matching, the competencies are most important. And with the task of meaning construction, the skills of grouping, induction, deduction, synthesis, and abstracting are most important. However, the value of the individual skills and competencies varies by particular challenges presented by different types of messages.

What Are the Essential Skills of Media Literacy?

In working with the ideas of media literacy over the past three decades, I have found that there is a set of seven **skills** that are most useful as tools in recognizing meaning in media messages and in transforming those meanings into useful knowledge for individuals. These seven skills are analyzing, evaluating, grouping, inducing, deducing, synthesizing, and abstracting. Let's examine each of these in detail.

1. Analyzing

Analyzing is the breaking down of a message into meaningful elements. As we encounter media messages, we can simply accept a surface meaning for each message or we can dig deeper into the message itself by breaking it down into its fundamental components and examining how those components work together to deliver some intended meaning. For example, with a news story, we can accept what a journalist tells us or we can analyze the story for completeness. That is, we can break the story down into its *who, what, when, where, why,* and *how* to determine if the story is complete or not. The key to using the skill of analysis well is to select the most useful analytical dimensions. Another analytical dimension for news stories is bias, where we examine the components to pay attention to the credibility of each bit of information and the degree to which the sides of a controversy are presented in a balanced manner. Therefore, the key to using analysis well is to select the most useful analytical dimension, then to perceive how elements in the message array themselves on that analytical dimension.

2. Evaluating

Evaluating is the making of judgments about the value of elements. This judgment is made by comparing a message element to some standard. When we encounter opinions expressed by experts in media messages, we could simply memorize those opinions and make them our own. Or we could take the information elements in the message and compare them to our standards. If those elements meet or exceed our standards, we conclude that the message—and the opinion expressed there—is good; but if the elements fall short of our standard, then we judge the message to be unacceptable. Therefore, the key to using the skill of evaluation well is to select the most useful and appropriate standards.

3. Grouping

Grouping is the determining of which elements are alike in some way, then determining how a group of elements are different from other groups of elements. The key to applying the grouping skill well relies on employing the most useful classification rules. The media tell us what classification rules are, so if we accept their classification rules, we will end up with the groups they want us to use. But if we make the effort to determine which classification rules are the best ways for us to organize our perceptions of the world, we will end up with groupings that have more meaning and more value for us.

4. Inducing

Inducing is the inferring of a pattern across a small number of elements, then generalizing that pattern to all elements in the larger set. We see examples of induction all the time—some good examples and some not so good. One example is a public opinion poll. Surveyors ask a few hundred people a question and then generalize the results to the entire population. If the surveyors use a sample of people that represent the entire population, then this use of induction is good. However, if surveyors sample only one particular kind of person, then it is misleading to generalize their findings to the entire population, which is composed of all kinds of people.

We use induction in our everyday lives when we make a few observations, perceive a tentative pattern across those observations, then generalize. For example, we might get sick and go to the emergency room for treatment and have to wait several hours before being seen by a doctor. We get angry and claim that the entire health care system is overburdened and that everyone has to wait too long to get medical care.

5. Deducing

Deducing is using general principles to explain particulars, typically with the use of syllogistic reasoning. A well-known syllogism is: (1) All men are mortal (general principle). (2) Socrates is a man (particular observation). (3) Therefore, Socrates is mortal (conclusion reached through logical reasoning).

The starting place for deductive reasoning is our general principles. If our general principles are accurate, then we are likely to reach good conclusions. But when we have faulty general principles, we will end up explaining particular occurrences in a faulty manner. One general principle that most people hold to be true is that the media, especially television, have a very strong negative effect on other people. They have an unrealistic opinion that the media cause other people to behave violently. Some people believe that if you allow PSAs (public service announcements) on TV about using condoms, children will learn that it is permissible and even a good thing to have sex. This is clearly an overestimation. At the same time, people *under*estimate the influence the media have on them. When they are asked if they think the media have any effect on them personally, 88% say no. These people argue that the media are primarily channels of entertainment and diversion, so they have no negative effect on them. The people who believe this say that they have watched thousands of hours of crime shows and have never shot anyone or robbed a bank. Although this may be true, this argument does not fully support the claim that the media have no effect on them; this argument is based on the false premise that the media only trigger high-profile, negative, behavioral effects that are easy to recognize. But there are many more types of effects, such as giving people the false impression that crime is a more serious problem than it really is or that most crime is violent.

6. Synthesizing

Synthesizing is the assembling of elements into a new structure. This is an essential skill we use when building and updating our knowledge structures. As we take in new information, it often does not fit into an existing knowledge structure, so we must adapt that knowledge structure to accommodate the new information. Thus the process of synthesis is using our new media messages to keep reformulating, refining, and updating our existing knowledge structures.

7. Abstracting

Abstracting is creating a brief, clear, and accurate description capturing the essence of a message in a significantly smaller number of words than the message itself. Thus when we are describing a media message to someone else or reviewing the message in our own minds, we use the skill of abstracting. The key to using this skill well is to be able to capture the "big picture" or central idea of the media message in as few words as possible.

These seven skills are the tools we use to create, alter, and update our knowledge structures. We use these tools to sort through the flood of information to find those key bits we need for some purpose, then transform those bits in some way (judge their worth, look for a pattern, or draw a conclusion) so we can fit them into a meaningful knowledge structure. Skills are like muscles; the more you exercise them, the stronger they get. Without practice, skills become weaker.

III. Chapter Review

- There are many definitions of media literacy in the large scholarly literature. Most of those definitions share four ideas:

  o Media literacy is broad to include all messages from all media.

  o Media literacy focuses both on protecting and empowering.

  o Media literacy is a continuum, not a category.

  o Media literacy can be improved.

- Across those definitions of media literacy, the most prevalent components mentioned are skills, knowledge structures, and personal locus.

  o Skills are tools for accessing information, processing meaning, then creating and maintaining knowledge structures.

o   Knowledge structures are maps of information that show how things are related to one another; this structure of information provides a guide to selecting new information and making meaning of it.

o   Personal locus is composed of an individual's goals and drives that serve to guide and energize the person to seek out particular messages and process their meaning.

- Competencies are relatively simple to acquire and are categorical; that is, either a person has a competency or does not. In contrast, skills are performances that array along a wide continuum of difficulty. Skills require work to acquire and practice to improve.

- There are seven essential skills of media literacy: analyzing, evaluating, grouping, inducing, deducing, synthesizing, and abstracting.

Importance of Skills

We are all confronted daily with the problem of information saturation. The human mind has automatic mechanisms that help us navigate through this constant flood of information without drowning, but these automatic mechanisms run outside our awareness. If we want to control how we navigate our way through this tide of information, then we need particular skills. The better we are able to use these skills, the more control we will exercise over exposure to messages, how we access meaning from those messages, and how we use those meanings to enlarge our understanding of the world and ourselves.

I. The Media Challenge

We are living in a culture shaped by a constant flood of information. Because we were born into this information culture, we take much of it for granted. As the size of the information flow grows at an accelerating rate each year, we unconsciously adapt without really thinking through what those adaptations mean. So in this section, I will first help you understand the enormous size of this flood of information. Then I will show you how we have been unconsciously adapting to this growth.

Flood of Information

With the widespread use of each new mass medium, the amount of information flowing into our culture has increased. Furthermore, the rate of those increases has been accelerating, especially over the last several decades with the pervasiveness of the digital media.

As for the printed word, we now have more than 140 million book titles in existence, and another 1,500 new book titles are published throughout the world each day. Visual messages also proliferate. Hollywood releases more than 700 hours of feature films each year, which adds to its base of more than 100,000 hours of films studios have already released in previous years. Commercial television stations generate about 48 million hours of video messages every year worldwide and radio stations send out 65.5 million hours of original programming each year. As large as these numbers are, they represent only the contribution of information from traditional mass media.

Growth Is Accelerating

Not only are we already saturated with media messages, the rate of that saturation is growing at an accelerating pace. More information has been generated since you were born than the sum total of all information throughout all recorded history up until the time of your birth. And the rate continues to accelerate! In 2012, Silver estimated that the amount of information was doubling every year and by now the rate of growth is even higher.

The really dramatic acceleration in the growth of information in our culture has been coming from the newer mass media that disseminate information using the Internet, which has grown so large in a few short decades that no one knows how big it really is. Google has been attempting to index all the webpages available on the Internet, and that index has now reached over 60 billion webpages on its 900,000 company servers (WorldWideWebSize.com, 2019). However, Google has estimated that the Internet is likely to be over 130 trillion webpages (Schwartz, 2016), which means that Google has been able to index only 0.05% of the total Internet. Even Google cannot keep up with the flood of information into our culture.

How is it that so much information is now being produced? One reason is that there are now more people producing information than ever before. Half of all the scientists who have ever lived are alive today and producing information. Also, the number of people in this country who identify themselves as musicians has more than doubled in the last four decades, the number of artists has tripled, and the number of authors has increased fivefold (U.S. Census Bureau, 2017).

Another—and even more important—reason for the accelerating growth of information in our culture is that much of it is being produced by nonprofessionals. Now, we all create information every day and make it widely available, because we now have easy-to-use platforms to create and share information. You no longer need to be a musician to create songs; you can use GarageBand or other computer synthesizers. You don't need to be signed to a recording contract by a record company to distribute your songs. You don't need to work at a Hollywood film studio to be able to produce videos and widely disseminate them. You can create videos on your smartphone, edit them easily, and disseminate them on a platform such as YouTube, which now has more than 1 billion videos available for viewing and users are uploading more than 300 new hours of video *every minute of every day* (YouTube, 2018). You can also be a journalist, a fiction writer, a photographer, or even a video game designer as a hobby and make your messages easily available to millions of people, just like professional artists. Or you could generate and share smaller forms of information such as e-mails and tweets. There are now 3.2 billion Internet users worldwide and they send and receive 300 billion e-mail messages each day; Twitter users generate more than 500 million tweets per day; and Facebook reports that 100 million photos are uploaded each and every day (Pingdom, 2019).

Each of us is adding to this information flow like never before. Tucker (2014) explains:

Between checking your phone, using GPS, sending e-mail, tweets, and Facebook posts, and especially streaming movies and music, you create 1.8 million megabytes a year. It's enough to fill nine CD-ROMs every day. The device-ification of modern life in the developed world is the reason why more than 90 percent of all the data that exists was created in just the last three years. (p. xv)

Tucker continues, "And it's growing exponentially, with 44 times as much digital information expected to be created in 2020 compared to 2009" (p. xvi).

High Degree of Exposure

The media are highly attractive, so we increase the time we spend with media messages each year. Over the last 3 decades, every new survey of media use has shown that people on average have been increasing their exposure time every year. For example, in 2010, people spent an average of 10 hours and 46 minutes with all forms of the media each day (eMarketer, 2014). By 2017, people were spending more time with the media than with anything else, with the average person spending 12 hours and 1 minute per day on media (eMarketer, 2017).

It is clear that the media are an extremely important part of our everyday lives. In our information-saturated culture, we are constantly connected to our friends, our society, and the entire world through the media.

How Do We Keep Up?

Multitasking

How do we keep up with all this information? One technique that many people use is multitasking. For example, a person can listen to recorded music, text friends, and watch video on a pop-up window all at the same time—thus experiencing 3 hours of media usage or exposure for each hour of clock time.

Multitasking, however, is not a good enough strategy for helping us keep up with the flood of information. If you wanted to view all the videos uploaded to YouTube in just 1 day, it would take you an entire year of viewing with no breaks and you would have to multitask by constantly watching 16 screens! While multitasking helps increase our exposure, it cannot help us keep up with even a tiny fraction of the media messages we are exposed to every day.

Although we are all saturated with information, and each year the media are more aggressive in seeking our attention, we are able to deal with it. How is this possible? The answer lies in the way the human brain is wired and programmed—its hardware and software.

Hardware

The most remarkable piece of hardware on Earth is the human brain. Although the human brain is relatively small (weighing only about 1 kilogram), it has a remarkable capacity to take in information from the five senses (sight, hearing, touch, taste, and smell); process all that information by filtering it or storing it; then making decisions that result in action. The human brain is composed of 100 billion neuron cells, which is the number of stars in the Milky Way (Storr, 2014). Each cell is linked by synapses to as many as 100,000 other cells. That means your brain has created over

500 trillion string-like fibers called axons and dendrites that connect with other neurons at junctions called synapses. "These synapses constantly form and dissolve, weakening, and strengthening in response to new experiences" (Haven, 2007, p. 22).

As the human brain is constantly monitoring the environment, thousands of neurons are receiving stimulation from thousands of other neurons and must decide whether to ignore the input or respond in some way by sending a signal to another specific neuron. "Somehow, through this freeway maze of links, loops, and electric traffic jams, we each manage to think, perceive, consider, imagine, remember, react, and respond" (Haven, 2007, p. 22).

Software

How does this complex piece of hardware know what to do? The answer to this question is that the brain has been programmed to fulfill certain functions. This software tells the brain how to function, much like the software on your computers tells them what functions to perform and how to perform those functions.

Some of this software has been programmed into the brain before birth. For example, this prebirth software guides the brain's constant monitoring of automatic bodily functions such as the performance of the organs (heart, lungs, kidneys, etc.) to keep them functioning properly. The brain also has been programmed to monitor a person's environment for threats. For example, the orienting reflect directs the brain to pay attention to the environment for sudden changes like loud noises; when a potential threat is identified, the brain creates an attentional state that forces the person to examine the thing that triggered the attention to determine whether it is an actual threat or not. Also, the brain has been hard-wired with a fight-or-flight reflex so that when a potential threat is encountered, the body is automatically made ready (increased heart rate and blood pressure) to either fight off the threat or run away to safety.

In addition to the prebirth software that helps us maintain physical well-being, we are also born with software that enhances our social well-being. For example, scientists believe all humans are born with the capacity to communicate with other humans by expressing their meaning for things and accessing the thoughts of others. Although humans are born with the software that provides them with the capacity to learn and use language, we all must learn the language of our culture through experience; this is why humans have developed thousands of different languages. Thus, being human is a combination of using our innate programming (prebirth programmed software) as the potentials and then maximizing the development of those potentials through how we manage our experiences.

As we accumulate experiences in life, our minds accumulate additional programming that tells our brains how to perform additional functions, like math and logical reasoning; how to work through moral problems; how to control one's emotions; and how to expand and grow one's skills that would lead to rewarding careers and relationships. This additional programming initially comes from one's parents and siblings. It also comes from one's contact with cultural institutions, such as education, religion, politics, and government. It comes from one's friends, acquaintances, and even one's enemies. And it comes from the mass media. All of this additional programming shapes how we make decisions in our everyday world about what to wear, what to eat, what is important, how to act, and how to spend our resources of time and money. This programming is constantly running in our unconscious minds in the form of automatic routines.

Automatic Routines

The human mind can be wondrously efficient. It can perform many everyday tasks quickly by using **automatic routines,** which are sequences of thoughts and behaviors that we learn from experience then apply again and again with little effort. Once you have learned a sequence—such as tying your shoes, brushing your teeth, driving to school, or playing a song on the guitar—you can perform it over and over again with very little effort compared to the effort it took you to learn it in the first place.

As we learn to do something, we are writing the instructions like a computer code in our minds. That code then runs automatically in our unconscious minds and serves to guide us through the task with very little thought or effort. To illustrate, recall your experience in first learning to type. You had to think of the individual letters in each word, think about which key controlled which letter, and then command a finger to press the correct key. It took you a long time to type out each word. But now after much practice, your fingers (or thumbs) move over the keyboard quickly as you type out messages in seconds. Now when you message someone, you think only about the message while not having to think at all about the task of typing.

Psychologists refer to this automatic processing of information as **automaticity**. Automaticity is a mental state where our minds operate without any conscious effort from us. We encounter almost all media messages in a state of automaticity; that is, we put our minds on "automatic pilot" where our minds automatically filter out almost all message options. I realize that this might sound strange, but think about it. We cannot possibly consider every possible message and consciously decide whether to pay attention to it or not. There are too many messages to consider. Over time, we have developed automatic routines that guide this filtering process very quickly and efficiently so we don't have to spend much, if any, mental effort.

To illustrate this automatic processing, consider what you do when you go to the supermarket to buy food. Let's say you walk into the store with a list of 25 items you need to buy, and 15 minutes later you walk out of the store with your 25 items. In this scenario, how many decisions have you made? The easy answer is to say 25 decisions, because you made a separate decision to buy each of your 25 items as you put each item into your cart. But what about all the items you *decided not to buy*? The average supermarket today has about 40,000 items on its shelves. So you actually made 40,000 decisions in the relatively short time you were in the supermarket—25 decisions to buy the 25 products and all those other decisions not to buy the remaining 39,975 products. How did you accomplish such an extensive task in such a short period of time? You relied on automatic routines. See how these automatic routines govern your buying habits?

Our culture is a grand supermarket of media messages. Those messages are everywhere whether we realize it or not, except that there are far more media messages in our culture than there are products in any supermarket. In our everyday lives—like when we enter a supermarket—a program is loaded into our mind that tells it what to look for and automatically filters out the rest. This automatic processing guides most, but certainly not all, of our media exposures. With automatic processing, we experience a great deal of media messages without paying any attention to them. Every once in a while something in the message or in our environment triggers our conscious attention to a media message. To illustrate this, imagine yourself driving in your car and you have music playing through your car's sound system but your attention is on the conversation you are having with your friend who is seated next to you. Then your favorite song starts playing, and your attention shifts from the conversation to the music. Or perhaps your conversation is interrupted when your friend notices that the radio is playing her favorite song and she starts singing along with the music. In both scenarios, you are being exposed to a stream of media messages from your car sound system without paying conscious attention to them, but then something happens to trigger your conscious attention to the music.

There are advantages and disadvantages to automaticity. The huge advantage of automatic processing is efficiency. When the filtering software is running automatically, it is making thousands of decisions for us without requiring us to expend any effort.

There are, however, some significant disadvantages. When we rely exclusively on our automatic routines, we get into a rut and miss out on paying attention to many messages that may be highly useful to us; we never know what we are missing. When our minds are on automatic pilot, we may be missing a lot of messages that might be helpful or enjoyable to us. We might not have programmed all the triggers we need to help us get out of automatic processing when a potentially useful message comes our way. Returning to the supermarket example from above, let's say you are very health conscious. Had you been less concerned with efficiency when you went into the supermarket, you would have considered a wider range of products and read their labels for ingredients. Not all low-fat products have the same fat content; not all products with vitamins added have the same vitamins or the same proportions. Or perhaps you are very price conscious. Had you been less concerned with efficiency, you would have considered a wider variety of competing products and looked more carefully at the unit pricing so you could get more value for your money. When we are *too* concerned with efficiency, we lose opportunities to expand our experience and to put ourselves in a position to make better decisions that can make us healthier, wealthier, and happier.

Another disadvantage is that over the long run we start to experience message fatigue. When we feel overwhelmed with too many media messages, we try to protect ourselves even more by narrowing down our focus and thus filtering out even more messages. Eventually we end up exposing ourselves to the same type of message over and over, and the value of each message keeps decreasing and we lose the ability to concentrate. In 1971, the Nobel Prize–winning economist Herbert Simon observed that "a wealth of information creates a poverty of attention" (Angwin, 2009, p. 239). This is illustrated by a study where experimenters set up a jam tasting table in a food store. Half the time, they offered 6 jams and the other half the time they offered 24 jams. While the table with more jams attracted 50% more visitors and tasters, the table with fewer jams stimulated more sales. Among the visitors to the table with the larger number of jams, only 3% bought some jam, while among the visitors to the table with the smaller number of jams, 30% bought some jam (Anderson, 2006). The lesson here is that while choice is attractive, too much choice can paralyze us into inaction. When we feel overwhelmed, we rely more and more on automatic routines and this leads us into a deeper and deeper rut of doing the same things over and over.

II. Types of Problems

Fully Specified Versus Partially Specified Problems

You probably have heard the phrase "Once you understand the problem, you are already halfway to a solution." This saying is true in the sense that the more clearly a problem can be understood, the easier it is to move toward a solution.

It also helps to know the type of problem—that is, whether it is a **fully specified problem** or a **partially specified problem**. To illustrate the difference between fully specified and partially specified problems, consider this:

$$6 + 18 = \underline{\hspace{2cm}}$$

If you understand that "6" and "18" represent numbers with particular values and that the symbol "+" means addition, then the problem has provided you with enough information that you can arrive at a solution of 24 with ease and have confidence that your solution to this problem is the correct one. If you have some training in arithmetic, then this problem is fully specified. The combination of what you already know along with the information presented in the problem itself is enough for you to solve the problem, arriving at one and only one correct answer.

Now consider this problem:

$$Y + Z = 24$$

This problem has two unknowns (Y and Z), so there is not enough information to arrive at one solution with confidence. You could answer 6 and 18, while I might answer 12 and 12. We would both be right. There are also many other correct answers to this problem. But this does not mean that there are no wrong answers, because there are also many wrong answers. The purpose of education is to train us so we can bring enough information to problems to make them fully specified and therefore allow us to solve them by arriving at a single correct answer. However, we are constantly challenged with partially specified problems in our everyday lives.

How can we recognize partially specified problems? We need to look for one of three characteristics. The first characteristic is that there is not one clearly best endpoint to the process; that is, several people could all solve the problem with different solutions. All solutions could be correct but none is more correct than the others, so we are not sure which is *the* solution. This is illustrated above with the problem of $Y + Z = 24$.

A second characteristic that indicates a partially specified problem is an unclear beginning point. We have some information but we are really not sure which elements in that information set are going to be useful and which are not. An example of this is what takes place in detective stories. While there is a clear ending point (discovery of the perpetrator), the beginning point is unclear. The detectives are missing important clues or they have some clues but they don't know which of those clues are useful and which are "red herrings," so the detectives fumble around chasing false leads, which deflect them away from arriving at the correct solution. Of course, in fictional stories, the detectives stick with it until they figure out which clues *are* more valid, and this gives them the traction they need to begin moving forward toward solving the crime.

A third characteristic that indicates a partially specified problem is an incomplete process that links a clear beginning point with a clear goal as a solution to the problem; that is, there are steps missing that are needed to arrive at one solution. This is rather like a professor giving students some information to begin a project and giving them some examples for what the outcome of the project should look like (such as a term paper) but then not telling them the full set of steps to go from the beginning to the outcome successfully. There are steps missing. Another example of this third characteristic is trying to solve the problem of where to go for dinner tonight. There are many good restaurants, each with its own advantages and disadvantages (quality of food, service, atmosphere, price, distance from home, parking, etc.). It is like comparing apples and oranges when considering the advantages and disadvantages of each. Usually there are many solutions to this problem, but which one is best? What is missing is an articulation of the criteria for choosing one solution over the rest. Perhaps restaurant A has the best food, restaurant B has the best service, restaurant C has the best atmosphere, and restaurant D has the best prices. All of these restaurants are good choices but for different reasons. What is missing in the solution process is the criterion that should be used. If you have little money, then price is the most important criterion; restaurant D is thus not just one of four possible solutions, it is the best solution. Thus when we have an unclear method of assessing the value of outcomes, we find ourselves stuck with a partially specified problem.

Partially specified problems are not uncommon. We often encounter them in our everyday lives. With most of these everyday partially specified problems, we quickly come up with a solution then move on. The consequences of being wrong are usually trivial. However, when we must make a decision on a problem that has major consequences for our lives and that problem is partially specified, we may agonize over the solution. As we try to solve that type of problem, we know that we have no model to follow, so we ask other people what they would do. If we find that most people would do the same thing, we usually use that advice and do the same thing also. However, if we find all kinds of suggestions as advice, then we must make some assumptions and engage our feelings.

The key difference between fully and partially specified problems is how much relevant information the problem itself provides. If it provides a complete set of information like with the first example above, then we can use a learned algorithm (in this case, the arithmetic algorithm of simple addition). With partially specified problems, algorithms are not enough; we also need heuristics.

Algorithms Versus Heuristics

There are some standard rules that can be provided to you for traversing just about any problem-solving path. These are called **algorithms**. Algorithms are formulas or lists of steps. Algorithms are the rules that tell us what to do step by step. If the problem is fully specified, then the algorithm will tell us all we need to know in order to solve the problem with confidence. An algorithm is a procedure for solving a problem, which (if followed accurately) guarantees that we will find a workable solution to the problem in a finite number of steps.

Computers follow algorithms to progress down a problem-solving path. If the problem is fully specified, the computer can quickly solve the problem. But if the problem is only partially specified, the algorithm does not provide enough guidance to complete the problem-solving process.

Humans also use algorithms to solve problems. If the problem is fully specified, then the algorithm provides enough guidance to complete the problem-solving process. With partially specified problems, algorithms still help, but these algorithms rarely take you all the way to a solution because they leave out parts of the solution path; that is, they are too general to provide the full amount of guidance for all particular problems. How do we bridge these gaps along the problem-solving path? We employ what cognitive psychologists call heuristics.

Heuristics are suggestions about how we should go about exercising our judgment. They are guidelines or recommendations more than rules or prescriptions. While algorithms provide a complete sequence of rules for moving logically to a problem's one correct solution, heuristics are suggestions for ways of proceeding to a solution under conditions of uncertainty. Heuristics can lead you to solutions, but there are no guarantees.

In order for heuristics to work, the problem solver needs to be more active and more creative. The problem solver needs to regard the heuristic as only a suggestion—a suggestion that requires the problem solver to use things like lateral thinking, metaphor, personal judgment, and even intuition.

Lateral Thinking. We are taught to solve problems by thinking sequentially beginning at the first step and continuing one step at a time all the way to the one solution at the end of the path, which is called **vertical thinking**. This vertical form of thinking is concerned with achieving a solution using a logical process. It is efficient when it keeps us on track toward a goal and prevents us from wandering into unproductive or incorrect thought processes.

We can often get stuck when we use vertical thinking, especially with partially specified problems. Sometimes we are moving smoothly down the problem-solving path as we systematically use a step-by-step procedure as specified in an algorithm, but then we suddenly run into a barrier that prevents us from moving logically to the next step. When this happens, we need to try a different approach such as lateral thinking. **Lateral thinking** involves brainstorming and creative thinking as we try to figure out a way around the barrier.

Lateral thinking is a way of restructuring old patterns to gain new insights. It is not as useful in generating the one "right" answer as much as it is helpful in leading us to brainstorm and think about fresh approaches. Therefore, lateral thinking is most useful when we are stuck and logic does not help us move toward a solution to a problem.

Metaphors. The essence of a **metaphor** is its evocative power to help us understand one thing in terms of another. We encounter something new and in order to see its nature, we liken it to something with which we are familiar. For example, let's say we run into a barrier in solving a problem and don't know how to proceed when our path is blocked. We could use the game of football as a metaphor. If we can't run the ball straight ahead, then we need to run around the end; once we turn the corner, we can see some daylight and run for the end zone. Or we could throw a long pass. These metaphors get us thinking about either moving around the barrier or jumping over it in some way. We look for connections between the game of football and our present situation. By making these connections, we can help break out of the place where we are stuck.

Oftentimes, metaphors we try might not be appropriate and sometimes we will not be able to help us find insight in the connections we make. But the value of metaphors is still there; that is, playing with metaphors keeps our thinking fresh by helping us perceive things from different perspectives. And perhaps one of these perspectives might suggest an innovative solution path.

Some educators regard metaphors as the key to knowledge, because all new knowledge is first encountered in terms of our experience with our existing knowledge. Again, this is why having good knowledge structures is so important. When we encounter new information, we can search our existing knowledge structures for something that looks and acts like the new information. Something that "looks or acts like something else" is a metaphor. Metaphors then give us the insight to understand something new in terms of our understanding of something old.

Personal Judgment. Some tasks, like spelling, are lower-order tasks, because if you follow the rules you can complete the task. If you memorize that *chair* is spelled c-h-a-i-r, you can finish the spelling without having to exercise any **personal judgment**. But if I asked you to spell a word that you had not memorized, you would not have much confidence in being prepared to complete the task well. Instead, you may feel like you must make a wild guess. However, often we do not have to risk a wild guess but instead can use good judgment to generate an educated guess. We can use what we know (about translating sounds into letters, the spelling of other English words, and other guides such as "i before e except after c") to construct a reasonable spelling. It requires judgment to translate rules that are designed for one kind of problem to try to solve a different kind of problem.

Intuition. The use of heuristics is also helped by intuition. **Intuition** engages the emotions and helps us guess at what could be plausible solutions without having to go through a systematic process. Often the insightful guess or the creative leap to a tentative conclusion can help us see a reasonable solution that we could not see by reason alone. We need to explore our hunches. However, we should not rely solely on hunches or intuition to solve problems, especially important ones. Intuition is one of many useful tools, but not the only tool of an educated person.

To summarize this distinction, algorithms are relative simple formulas or prescriptions that tell us how to go about solving fully specified problems. Heuristics are also guides, but they are not simple or complete. Whereas algorithms are rules, heuristics are suggestions. Algorithms give us the steps of how to apply our skills in solving a problem. Heuristics tell us what to think about when we encounter gaps in that process, and this serves to help us shift our perspective, see the problem in a new way, construct elements to help us bridge the gaps, then eventually complete the problem-solving process. To be good problem solvers, we need to be able to apply both algorithms and heuristics. The stronger our skills, the better we will be able to use both.

The Problem-Solving Process

If partially specified problems are missing information, does this mean we can never solve them? No, of course not. But in order to solve them, we need to take a different perspective than we do with fully specified problems. We cannot approach a partially defined problem and expect to solve it as if it were a fully specified problem.

Problem solving is a process that begins with an awareness of a challenge facing you. You search your mind for information relevant to the challenge. If you find enough information, it is likely that you have a fully specified problem and that you have already arrived at a solution by following what is called an algorithm. But if you do not have enough information to arrive at a solution, you must search out more information. And even when you have accessed a great deal of information, there are times when you still cannot solve the problem because you are not sure what to do with the information; that is, the formula you are using to solve the problem has some missing parts. In this situation, you need more than an algorithm; you also need some heuristics.

If we are to be successful in solving partially specified problems, we cannot be stopped by the gaps where we don't have enough information. Instead, we need to use the information we have to construct the additional information we need, then use that newly constructed information to bridge the gaps and keep us progressing toward a solution. Heuristics can help us construct those missing pieces by providing us with guidelines that tell us what to think about as we build the bridges over the gaps.

Does this mean that this process of solving challenging problems is idiosyncratic? Yes, in the sense that each challenging problem is different in what it leaves unspecified. Thus no one can provide you with a set of rules—an algorithm—that lays out a complete set of steps to solve any problem. Instead algorithms provide rules for general processes; they give you a generic structure solving different kinds of problems. You will also need to use heuristics. The heuristics are less formal, less constraining, and less directive than are algorithms. They give you freedom to try different things in different sequences.

The heuristics we use are influenced by context (our knowledge structures); because different people have different knowledge structures, they use slightly different heuristics and thereby end up with different solutions. Heuristics rely more on lateral thinking than vertical thinking. They nudge us to be more creative by suggesting metaphors. They sanction the use of individual human judgment and intuition, rather than relegating these characteristics to second class status in problem solving.

Skills are typically important in applying algorithms. The more highly developed our skills are, the more efficiently we can use algorithms. But even more importantly, skills are essential with heuristics, because heuristics require us to think more deeply and creatively about how to solve partially specified problems.

III. The Development of Skills

There are three factors that explain where a person's level of skill is: **natural abilities, maturation**, and **self-improvement**. The first two of these factors occur naturally; that is, we are born with certain abilities and those abilities develop on their own without much effort required from us. The third factor—self-improvement—requires conscious effort.

Natural Abilities

We are born with certain natural aptitudes that can shape the development of our knowledge style. Some of these abilities are cognitive in nature, while others are more emotional in nature.

Cognitive Abilities

Some of us have higher IQs, some of us are naturally more field independent, and some of us seem to have been born with higher creative abilities and a tendency to think laterally. Other people have innate learning disabilities, such as dyslexia, that make it much harder for them to process information.

Some people can memorize facts very well, while others cannot. Some are able to think about problems in many different ways, while others seem stuck in one perspective when they view a problem. Some people are continually playing with information by creating new categories and looking for patterns, while other people either try to ignore information or try to find quick and easy ways to deal with it. Knowledge styles are characterized primarily by four cognitive abilities: field dependency, type of intelligence, type of thinking, and conceptual differentiation.

Field Dependency. Perhaps the most important characteristic in a person's cognitive style is field dependency. Think of **field dependency** as your natural ability to distinguish between the signal and the noise in any message. Noise is the chaos of symbols and images. Signal is the information that emerges from the chaos. People who are highly field dependent get stuck in the field of chaos—seeing all of the details but missing the patterns and the "big picture," which is the signal. Field-independent people are able to sort quickly through the field to identify the elements of importance and ignore the distracting elements.

For example, when watching a story during a television news show, field-independent people will be able to identify the key information of the who, what, when, where, and why of the story. They will quickly sort through what is said, the graphics, and the visuals to focus on the essence of the event being covered. People who are field dependent will perceive the same key elements in the story but will also pay an equal amount of attention to the background elements of how the news anchors are dressed, their hairstyles, their make-up, the color of the graphics, and so on. To the field-dependent person, all of these elements are of fairly equal importance, so they are as likely to remember the trivial as they are to remember the main points of the story. This is not to say that field-dependent people retain more information because they pay attention to more; to the contrary, field-dependent people retain less information, because the information is not organized well and is likely to contain as much noise (peripheral and tangential elements) as signal (elements about the main idea).

Let's try one more example of this natural ability. Have you ever had to read a long novel and gotten so lost about 100 pages into it that you had to quit in frustration? You may have felt that just when the author was getting the story going with one set of characters, he or she would switch to a different setting at a different time with a totally new set of characters. This may have been happening every few pages! There were too many characters talking about too many different things. You were overwhelmed by all the detail and could not make sense of the overall story. This indicates that the novelist was making demands on you to be much more field independent than you could be as you read the novel. People who are much more field independent are able to see through all the details and recognize a thematic pattern of some sort, then use that thematic pattern as a tool to sort through all the details about characters, settings, time, dialogue, and action in order to direct their attention efficiently to those elements that are most important.

In our information-saturated culture, we are constantly forced to make filtering decisions when those messages that are regarded as signal are filtered into our consciousness while those messages that are regarded as noise are filtered out. Most of this filtering is done rapidly and unconsciously while our programmed mental codes run automatically. If those codes have been programmed by media producers, then those producers are defining what is important—thus what is important to them gets filtered in, while much of what may be important to us gets filtered out. This is why it is important for us to periodically examine the codes and make adjustments that give us more control over this filtering.

Type of Intelligence. It is helpful to make a distinction between two types of intelligence: **crystalline intelligence** and **fluid intelligence**. One type of intelligence is called crystalline, which is the ability to memorize facts. Highly developed crystalline intelligence gives us the facility to absorb the images, definitions, opinions, and agendas of others.

The other type of intelligence is fluid, which is the ability to be creative and see patterns in complex sets of facts. Highly developed fluid intelligence gives us the facility to challenge what we see on the surface, to look deeper and broader, and to recognize new patterns.

Type of Thinking. Most people are what are called vertical thinkers (recall that this idea was introduced earlier in this chapter). Vertical thinking is systematic, logical thinking that proceeds step by step in an orderly progression. This is the type of thinking we need to learn the basic introductory information on any topic. We need to be systematic when we are trying to learn basic arithmetic, spelling, and dates in history.

As we discussed earlier, there is another type of thinking called lateral thinking. Lateral thinking, in contrast, does not proceed step by step in the usual vertical manner. Instead, when confronted with a problem, the lateral thinker jumps to a new and quite arbitrary position, then works backward and tries to construct a logical path between this new position and the starting point. Lateral thinkers are more intuitive and creative. They reject the standard beginning points to solving problems and instead begin with an intuitive guess, a brainstorming of ideas, or proposed solution "out of the blue." The lateral thinker works backward from innovative conclusions to the beginning of a problem. Lateral thinkers tend to arrive at a solution to a problem that other thinkers would never arrive at because they are constrained by a lock-step form of thinking.

Few people have a natural aptitude for lateral thinking. Those who have it use it often. Many inventors and scientists usually produce a string of new ideas, not just one. For example, Thomas Edison invented so many things that by the end of his life he had over 1,300 patents in the areas of the telegraph, telephone, phonograph, movie camera, and projectors. This suggests that there is a capacity for generating new ideas that is better developed in some people than in others. This capacity does not seem to be related to sheer intelligence but more to a particular way of thinking. There are smart and not-so-smart lateral thinkers, just like there are smart and not-so-smart vertical thinkers.

There are advantages and disadvantages to both forms of thinking. Vertical thinkers tend to do best at solving traditional problems for which the solutions can be learned. However, when their traditional methods of solving problems break down and they reach a dead end, they are stuck and have nowhere to go. In contrast, lateral thinkers can often be flighty and may come up with many unique ideas; however, none of those ideas may work or be feasible ways of addressing a problem. When others are stuck at a dead-end of thinking, it is the lateral thinkers that break through the barriers. People who are good at both and who know when to try each approach are, of course, the most successful problem solvers.

It is easier to teach vertical thinking than lateral thinking, because vertical thinking is a process of systematically following steps and procedures. In contrast, lateral thinkers know how to approach things from a different and creative point of view; this is difficult to teach. Because it is easier to teach and evaluate the quality of vertical thinking, educational institutions focus much more on vertical thinking at the introductory level where you need to absorb the formulas and lists that authorities deem most important. However, once you get beyond this type of challenge, you will encounter more significant challenges where you will need to solve partially specified problems. You will need to move beyond memorizing information and instead look for fresh patterns, synthesize your own opinions, and project future trends. These more challenging tasks will frequently present barriers that can be circumvented only through lateral thinking.

Conceptual Differentiation. **Conceptual differentiation** refers to how people group and classify things. People who classify objects into a large number of mutually exclusive categories exhibit a high degree of conceptual differentiation. In contrast, people who use a small number of categories have a low degree of conceptual differentiation.

Related to the number of categories is category width. People who have few categories to classify something usually have broad categories so as to contain all types of messages. For example, if a person only has three categories for all media messages (news, ads, and entertainment), then each of these categories must contain a wide variety of messages. In contrast, someone who has a great many categories would be dividing media messages into thinner slices (breaking news, feature news, documentary, commercial ads, public service announcements, action/adventure shows, sitcoms, game shows, talk shows, cartoons, and reality shows).

Emotional Abilities

A person's knowledge style is composed of more than purely cognitive abilities. It is important to recognize the role of emotional abilities. Some people are naturally excited by new information and have a strong drive to seek out more. However, other people feel exhaustion when experiencing new information, because they already feel overwhelmed. In the paragraphs below, I will illuminate three characteristics of emotional ability that contribute to a person's knowledge style. These are: emotional intelligence, tolerance for ambiguity, and impulsiveness.

Emotional Intelligence. Our ability to understand and control our emotions is called **emotional intelligence**. Emotional intelligence is thought to be composed of several related abilities, such as the ability to read the emotions of other people (empathy), the ability to be aware of one's own emotions, the ability to harness and manage one's own emotions productively, and the ability to handle the emotional demands of relationships.

People with stronger emotional intelligence have a well-developed sense of empathy; they are able to see the world from another person's perspective. The more perspectives people can access, the more emotional intelligence they have. Highly developed people are also more aware of their own emotions and understand what causes and alters them. These people are also less impulsive and are able to exercise more self-control. They can concentrate on the task at hand rather than becoming distracted by peripheral emotions. When we are higher developed emotionally, we are better able to understand how messages evoke feelings, and we can therefore seek out messages to enhance our emotional reactions.

Tolerance for Ambiguity. Every day, we encounter people and situations that are unfamiliar to us. To prepare ourselves for such situations, we have developed sets of expectations. What do we do when our expectations are not met and we are surprised? That depends on our tolerance level for ambiguity. People who have a low **tolerance for ambiguity** choose to ignore those messages that do not meet their expectations; they feel too confused or frustrated to work out the discrepancies. In contrast, those people who are willing to follow situations into unfamiliar territory that goes beyond their preconceptions have a high tolerance for ambiguity. Initial confusion does not stop them; instead it motivates them to search harder for clarity.

People with a high tolerance for ambiguity do not feel an emotional barrier that prevents them from examining messages more closely. They are willing to break any message down into components and make comparisons and evaluations in a quest to understand the nature of the message and to examine why their initial expectations were wrong. People who consistently attempt to verify their observations and judgments are called scanners, because they are perpetually looking for more information.

Nonimpulsiveness. **Nonimpulsiveness** refers to people's ability to control their emotions when dealing with information. Some people get swept away with negative emotions, such as frustration or anger. They cannot control their emotions, so they let negative emotions force them to make quick decisions so as to eliminate the negative drive. When people make quick decisions, their choices are usually not optimal. There is typically a trade-off between speed and accuracy. When we are impulsive, we make decisions very quickly and this moves us out of the uncomfortable emotion of stress. However, when we take our time and reflect, we usually make better decisions. People who take a long time and make few errors are reflective, and those who are quick and make many errors are impulsive.

How much time we take to make decisions is governed by our emotions. If we feel comfortable encountering new information and like to work through problems carefully, we are likely to act reflectively and take our time. However, if we feel a negative emotion (such as frustration), we tend to make decisions as quickly as possible in order to eliminate the negative emotional state.

As we encounter information throughout the course of our lives, our natural abilities (or deficiencies) make it easier (or more difficult) to deal with this information. Also, dealing with information becomes less difficult when we are at higher levels of maturation on a wide range of abilities. However, regardless of our innate abilities and our levels of maturation, there is another factor that arguably is most responsible for our knowledge style—that is, conditioning.

Maturation

Our innate abilities mature on their own early in our lives. This means that we get better at understanding more difficult concepts and in controlling our emotions. Much of this maturation happens outside our control or awareness. Children have difficulty comprehending certain ideas until their minds mature to a point where they are capable of understanding the nature of what they are doing. For example, you cannot teach a 1-year-old to add and subtract, no matter how good of a teacher you are. The child does not understand what adding and subtracting are and is not ready to learn these things at 1 year of age. However, over the next few years, the child's mind matures and becomes ready to learn these things.

The leading thinker about human cognitive development, Jean Piaget, observed that a child's mind matures from birth to about 12 years of age, during which time it goes through several identifiable stages. Other psychologists have examined how the human mind matures beyond the age of 12. Psychologists still have a lot to learn about how humans develop cognitively and emotionally throughout the entire lifespan. However, what we do know is that we continue to mature on all sorts of abilities throughout both childhood and adulthood and that those patterns of maturation differ across people. We also know that there are some things we can do to accelerate certain kinds of maturation and there are other things we don't do that can atrophy the process and keep us stuck at a low level of development for our entire adult lives.

Self-Improvement

All of us have the potential to continue developing our skills at any point in our lives. Regardless of our innate abilities, we can still get better. Once we have reached college, we cannot rely on maturation for improvement; our minds have matured to a point where maturation is no longer a barrier. Regardless of how we have been conditioned, we can take control of our futures. Even if we have been conditioned to believe we are not very smart, we can still improve. We can develop our skills on our own. To do so, we need to become committed to our improvement and we need to work on it.

IV. Chapter Review

- We live in an information-saturated culture.

  o In order to survive, we have developed automatic routines that help us navigate this flood of information.

  o These routines help us make decisions efficiently about what exposures to seek and how to process meaning from those messages.

  o These routines are composed of programming that has been designed by other people and institutions, so those routines may not be running in our best interest.

- The way we solve problems differs depending on whether the problems are fully specified or partially specified.

  o We depend on algorithms to solve fully specified problems so we can arrive at the one and only correct solution.

- o When we solve partially specified problems, algorithms help us get started but we also need to use heuristics.

- Our level of skills is determined by a combination of natural ability, maturation, and self-improvement efforts.

  - o We are all born with different combinations of natural abilities.

  - o Our abilities to use cognitive and emotional skills mature as we age throughout childhood.

  - o Beyond childhood, the most important determinant of people's levels of skill is traceable to their efforts at self-improvement.

Exercise 2.1 Recognizing Types of Problems

Which of the following are examples of fully specified problems and which are partially specified problems?

1. $(2 + 6 + X)/3 = 5$

2. $(6 + 4 + X)/2 = 3X$

3. $2 + X + Y = 10$

4. Train Number 1 leaves the station in City X at noon heading toward City Y, which is 1,000 miles away. Train Number 2 leaves City Y at 1:00 p.m. traveling toward City X. Both trains travel at 70 miles per hour. At what mile marker will the trains pass each other?

5. A red train leaves the station in City X at noon heading toward City Z at 60 miles per hour. At the same time, a blue train leaves City Z traveling at 80 miles per hour. City X and City Z are 560 miles apart. At what mile marker will the trains pass each other?

6. In a vote by a legislature, a bill gets 55 votes. Does it pass and become a law?

7. Joey is a 12-year-old boy who has just watched half an hour of wrestling on the World Wrestling Entertainment (WWE) network. His younger sister comes into the TV room, grabs the remote control, and changes the channel. Will Joey act aggressively toward her?

8. When will the U.S. economy get better?

* * * * * * *

Answers for Exercise 2.1

1. This is a fully specified problem. There is one unknown, X. The solution is 7.

2. This also is a fully specified problem. Although X shows up twice in the equation, X is only one unknown. The answer is 2.

3. This is a partially specified problem, because there are two unknowns.

4. This is a fully specified word problem. Because the trains travel at the same speed, they should be expected to meet halfway—at the 500-mile marker. However, Train 1 leaves an hour early, so they should pass each other 570 miles from City X.

5. This might look like a fully specified problem, but if you look closely, there is no information about where the blue train is headed. That is a crucial piece of information that is not provided. However, you could make this into a fully specified problem by learning that the blue train is indeed heading toward City X.

6. This is a partially specified problem, because it is missing two pieces of information. First, we are not told how many members there are in the legislature and whether the bill needs a majority, a plurality, or a certain percentage of the vote to pass. Second, we are not told if there are steps beyond the vote in order for the bill to become a law. Perhaps a member of an executive branch of the government needs to sign the bill; perhaps there needs to be a general election. However, you could make this into a fully specified problem by finding out what the rules are.

7. This is a partially specified problem. It is tempting to jump to the conclusion that Joey will scream at his sister and grab the remote control. But we don't know enough to conclude this. Perhaps the sister was assaulted by the neighborhood bully and has just come back from the doctor after getting her broken arm put in a cast. Joey is feeling protective over his sister and his anger flares up at the bully, not his sister. Or perhaps Joey was responsible for his sister's broken arm and he is feeling remorseful. You could move this more toward a fully specified problem by finding out more information about Joey and his sister.

8. This is a classic partially specified problem. There are hundreds of factors that influence the economy. Also, there are many economists who continually track these factors and make predictions, and most of those economists are wrong at any given time. Still it is a fascinating and important problem, so people continually address it. You can work to make it less partially specified by gathering information on the hundreds of factors over time and plotting trends. This will serve to reduce the ambiguity in the problem, but it will not take you all the way to a solution in which you can have 100% confidence.

Analyzing

Digging Into the Meaning and Structure of Media Messages

Analysis is the skill we use to examine an object in order to increase our understanding of that object. The **object** can be tangible (such as a building, a sandwich, an ocean, a crime scene) or intangible (such as an idea, a problem, a relationship, a plan, a memory). Because this is a book about media literacy skills, the objects we are most interested in analyzing are media messages.

The skill of analysis is the most fundamental of the seven skills illuminated in this book. Analysis is the most primary of these because an analysis of a media message is typically required to identify the elements that then become the raw materials that the other six skills require. Although the skill of analysis is needed as a prelude to engaging in tasks using the other six skills, it can also be conducted as a stand-alone that produces elements that have value without having to be used with other skills.

The terms *analyzing* and *searching* are often used as synonyms, but in this book they are used with distinct meanings. Although using the skill of analysis may sometimes involve searching, analysis is more than just searching. The process of **searching** is simply the looking for one particular **element** in a field of many elements, whereas **analysis** is a tool that is used to increase understanding about a **field of elements**. The field could be a physical location (such as your apartment) where you search for one particular element (such as your keys) that is somewhere among all the other elements in the field. In another example, let's say you are writing a term paper for a course and you need to find a particular fact. You search for that fact on the Internet, where the field is the total set of all informational elements spread out across all the webpages on the Internet. In these examples, you are conducting a search, not an analysis. When you search through your apartment for your keys, you are not concerned about increasing your understanding about the field of elements in your apartment; instead, you just want to find your keys. When you search the Internet for a particular fact, you are not concerned about increasing your understanding of the Internet. You do not care about how many webpages are indexed by the search engine you are using, the content of all of those webpages, or how those webpages are organized. You just want to find the one fact you need for your term paper. When you find the one thing you are searching for, you have successfully completed your search; however, this searching has not increased your understanding of the field, whether it be your apartment or the Internet. Thus, applying the skill of analysis is more involved than simply searching, because analysis is not limited to finding one element; the use of the skill of analysis is concerned with extending your understanding of the field of elements being analyzed.

I. The Analysis Algorithm

Using the skill of analysis essentially proceeds through four steps that I present here as an algorithm, which is a general guide for using the skill of analysis (Table 3.1). As I show you how to use this algorithm, notice that I am focusing on the object of media messages. However, the skill of analysis can be used on any object.

The first step in this analysis algorithm is to select an object to analyze. Second, you need to clarify your purpose for conducting an analysis of your chosen object. Third, select the most appropriate analytical dimension(s) to fulfill your acknowledged purpose. And fourth, use the selected analytical dimension(s) to identify the elements in the object that fulfill your purpose.

Step 1: Select an Object to Analyze

Selecting an object to analyze is typically triggered by curiosity. For example, let's say you are in a coffee shop when you hear a song that you have never heard before. You are curious about who the singer is so you click an

TABLE 3.1   **The Skill of Analyzing**

Purpose: To identify the elements within a message
Algorithm:

1. Select an object to analyze.
 	
   o   An object is a field of elements of interest.
   o   With media messages, objects are news stories, advertisements, photographs, songs, novels, short stories, video narratives, websites, e-mails, and so forth.
 	
2. Determine your purpose for the analysis.
 	
   o   Will you use a breadth approach?
   o   Will you use a depth approach?
   o   Will you use a combination approach?
 	
3. Select the most appropriate dimension(s) to fulfill your purpose.
 	
4. Use the analytical dimension to identify elements in the object.
 	
   o   If you are using a breadth approach, then identify the surface components that make up the object being analyzed.
   o   If you are using a depth approach, then identify the layers of elements that are used in the object to elaborate a particular component.
   o   If you are using a combination approach, then you will need to complete both a breadth and depth approach.

app on your smartphone and begin recording the song. After a few minutes, your app tells you the name of the song and who sings it. In this case, the app has done the analysis for you; that is, the app noticed enough elements in the song to be able to determine the name of the song and the singer.

Often we encounter media messages that stimulate our curiosity and could motivate an analysis. For example, perhaps you watched a video and afterward you wondered why you liked it so much. Or you notice a pop-up ad on your computer and are curious about where you could go to buy the product advertised and how much it will cost. Or you get a strange text message from a sender you do not recognize and wonder who sent it and whether it is spam. All of these are examples of you encountering a media message that stimulated your curiosity to find out more about particular elements that caught your attention in those messages. In order to act on this curiosity by increasing your understanding of those messages, you need to use the skill of analysis.

While all of the above examples are about a particular media message triggering curiosity in the short term, there are also many instances where you have been conditioned (or have conditioned yourself) over the long term to develop habits of curiosity that repeatedly trigger the need for analysis. For example, many people go online at the beginning of every day to learn what is happening either in their particular world (so they check social networking sites, phone messages, and texts) or the world in general (so they check news websites). Their continuing purpose is to find out the most recent developments in the lives of their friends, communities, towns, states, regions, country, and the world. Without consciously realizing it, they continually use their skill of analysis to identify the key bits of information presented in those messages that tell them what is new.

Someone may even require you to engage in analysis whether your curiosity is stimulated or not. For example, when you are enrolled in college courses, your professors will expect you to read textbooks and listen to their lectures in order to acquire important information. Many students simply assume that everything is important, so they highlight every word in the textbook and write down everything their professors say in lectures. But this is a highly inefficient and ineffective way to learn the course material, because not every word (or sentence or idea) in textbooks and lectures is equally important. Students who have a highly developed skill of analysis will be able to sift through all the elements in their fields of educational resources and identify those elements that are most important for conveying the essence of the knowledge being taught. In contrast, students whose skill of analysis is not well developed will instead try to memorize as many details as they can. This is very inefficient because it takes a great deal of time and effort to memorize a massive amount of detail; this strategy is also very ineffective because it prevents students from even perceiving the big picture of knowledge, much less using a big picture as a map to organize their acquisition of knowledge into a structure that will make it easier to remember the detail.

Therefore, the first step in any good analysis is to be aware of your need to analyze "something" and be clear about what that "something" is.

Step 2: Determine Your Purpose

Because every media message can be analyzed for different purposes, it is important that you clarify what your purpose is so you can conduct the type of analysis that will be most useful in fulfilling your needs for it. For example, let's take something relatively simple like an e-mail message you receive from a friend. You could analyze the message to identify the major ideas that your friend Chris is communicating to you (e.g., I'll meet you for dinner tonight at 7. Dress up. I'm bringing a friend named Pat.). You could analyze the same e-mail at a deeper level to try and understand what your friend Chris is saying "between the lines" by asking questions such as "Who is Pat?" "Why is Chris bringing Pat?" "Why do I need to dress up?" If your parents were analyzing this e-mail message, they would likely have a different purpose and therefore ask different questions. If English teachers were analyzing this message, they would likely be concerned with the elements of expression (grammar, punctuation, etc.). With any media message, there are typically many different reasons for conducting an analysis.

While clarifying your purpose is always keyed to the particulars of the object that you want to analyze, there is a general guideline I can provide. Think about how to focus your analysis either on breadth, depth, or a combination.

Breadth Approach

A **breadth approach** focuses your attention on using analysis to increase your understanding of the span of elements within the media message. You are not concerned about developing a deeper understanding of any of the elements in a message; instead you simply want to grasp a sense of how many elements the message presents, what those elements are, and how broad a span those elements cover. So your use of analysis of the message can stay on the surface and simply serve to identify the obvious elements expressed in the message being analyzed. For example, when you use a breadth approach to analyzing a news message, you are typically concerned with the informational elements (see Table 3.2). When you use a breadth approach to analyzing an entertainment story, you might be concerned only with the characters or perhaps with the plot points or settings. With advertising messages, you could analyze them for claims made about their advertised products. And with social media interactions, you could analyze them for the sequence of claims made by your friends as you text back and forth.

The breadth approach is especially useful in identifying sets and sequences in media messages. The elements generated by a breadth approach to analysis are especially useful as raw materials when we use the skill of abstracting.

TABLE 3.2   **Three Approaches for Analysis**

Object of Analysis	Breadth	Depth	Combination
News message	Set of informational components	Attribution of a fact	Relationships among facts
Entertainment story	Set of characters	Foundation for character's decisions	Relationships among characters
Advertising message	Claims about advertised product	Foundation for advertised claims	Relationship between problem and solution
Social media interaction	Sequence of comments	Foundation for comments	Relationship among comments

Depth Approach

A **depth approach** focuses your attention on using analysis to increase your understanding about a particular element among the set of elements presented in a media message. You are not concerned with identifying all the elements or components in a message; instead you focus on one particular element and need to "go deep" rather than wide. That is, you look for more than just the mention of the element; you look for subpoints and sub-subpoints about that element that are embedded in the message. In contrast to the breadth approach, your analysis does not stay on the surface of the message but digs deeper.

The breadth approach is especially useful in identifying information about attributions and foundations (see Table 3.2). For example, when you encounter a news story, you may become motivated to analyze the story because of a particular reported fact that is shocking to you. This stimulates you to question the veracity of that fact, so you are motived to analyze the message for evidence that the reported fact should be believed as accurate; you look for evidence that the journalist has presented to substantiate that fact. You look for quotations from experts. You look for explanations about how that fact might appear wrong but is actually accurate. Likewise you may be puzzled by a claim being made in advertising messages or in social media interactions, so you conduct an analysis in depth to look for elements that support that claim.

A depth approach to conducting an analysis is especially useful in preparing to use the skill of evaluation. The depth analysis identifies the elements in a media message that the message author has presented as evidence supporting a claim. You would then use these elements, which are produced by the analysis, as the raw materials when you use the skill of evaluation to make a judgment about whether that evidence is significant enough for you to judge the claim as receiving enough support or not.

Combination Approach

A **combination approach** focuses your attention on using analysis to increase your understanding about the full set of elements—both in scope and in depth—presented in a media message. Your analysis needs to follow the guidelines for both a breadth and depth approach in combination. As you can tell, this combination approach requires much more effort than either a breadth or depth approach by itself. For example, when you are preparing for an exam in a course, it is best to use a combination approach when analyzing the course material, such as from a textbook or a set of lectures. If you use only a breadth approach, you will end up memorizing all the components in the course but will have only superficial knowledge. If you use only a depth approach, you will end up understanding a few elements very well but you will miss many other elements.

The combination approach is especially useful in identifying information about relationships among the elements in the message (see Table 3.1). For example, let's say you encounter a news story about an event that will likely have a major effect on your life (such as an impending disaster in your neighborhood or the passage of legislation that will drastically change what you are allowed to do). When you analyze such a news story, you will likely want to know what all the major elements are (breadth analysis) so that you don't miss anything important, but you would also want to develop more than a superficial understanding about the meaning of each element and how all those elements are related to one another. As another example, let's say you observe how your favorite character is portrayed as behaving in an entertainment message such as a video series. You might become puzzled about why your favorite character seems to behave in a very unexpected way, so you conduct a depth-type analysis to first examine the foundation for the character's motivation. However, this alone might not satisfy your curiosity by explaining why your favorite character is behaving so strangely. You think there must be more going on in the story to explain the character's behavior, so you analyze other characters' foundations for their behavior and how their behaviors and motivations influence the behavior of your favorite character. This combination-type analysis (in-depth analysis across the full breadth of characters) will help you develop a much greater understanding of the dynamics of behavior through the entire video series.

A combination approach to conducting an analysis is especially useful in generating elements that are then the raw materials for using the skills of grouping, induction, and synthesis. When you use the skill of grouping, you first need to know what all the major elements are in a message; you also need to know enough about the characteristics of each of those elements so you can group all the elements on their characteristics. When you use the skill of induction, you first need to know what all the major elements are in a message; you also need to know enough about the characteristics of each of those elements so you have enough of a base of understanding to speculate well about how those elements form a pattern that can be generalized. When you use the skill of synthesis, you first need to know what all the major elements are in a message; you also need to know enough about the characteristics of each of those elements so you have enough of a base of understanding to know how all those elements work together, which elements do not work well together, and how to make corrections and fill in gaps in order to reformulate a better system of elements.

Step 3: Select the Analytical Dimension(s) That Will Fulfill Your Purpose

Once you are clear about your purpose, you then need to select an **analytical dimension** to use in conducting your analysis. Typically there are many analytical dimensions that could be used to analyze any kind of media message. For example, if you want to analyze a movie, you could analyze it by plot, by characters, by settings, by themes, and so on. Each of these is a different analytical dimension that would serve a different purpose. Selecting the most useful analytical dimension is relatively easy when you are clear about your purpose.

The key to completing this third step is to make sure that the analytical dimensions you select will fulfill your purpose for the analysis. There may be times when you have selected an analytical dimension you find fascinating but it has no relevance to your initial purpose for conducting the analysis. In this case, you could either (1) drop the selected dimension and find one that is more appropriate to achieve your initial purpose, or (2) change your purpose to fit with your selected dimension. Do not ignore this second option, because there are times when we learn that there is a better purpose for the analysis only when we are well into the analysis itself. Thus these two steps work in tandem.

Step 4: Identify the Elements

The fourth step is to use your selected analytical dimension(s) to identify the major elements in the object you are analyzing. When you conduct this step in the analysis, think about your analytical dimension as an array of choices. The more you know about the nature of your selected analytical dimension, the better you can use it efficiently in guiding your analysis.

If you are taking a breadth approach to analysis, then you need to use an analytical dimension that not only is relevant to your purpose but also includes a full set of components; the components become your choices. For example, let's say you are analyzing a news story on a controversial issue and your purpose is to increase your understanding about the various positions people hold on the controversy. You would likely start with an analytical dimension that included two categories of elements (pro and con), so you would analyze the news story to identify the elements that are reported to support the pro side and include those elements in one category. Then you would analyze the news story to identify the elements that are reported to support the con side and include those elements in the other category. In doing this step, you might find that some reported elements do not support either the pro or con side; in this case, perhaps the elements indicate that there is also a third position on the continuum in addition to the pro and con positions. Or perhaps there is a need to document a fourth or fifth position on the analytical dimension. If you have a lot of experience in thinking about this controversy, then you would likely start your analysis of the news story on the controversy with an already more highly developed analytical dimension (more than two simple pro and con dimensions). But if you are new to the controversy and have not thought much about it, then you can start with a simple analytical dimension with only two categories (pro and con) and elaborate it while conducting your analysis.

With a breadth approach, the analysis by components is completed when you have identified all the major components in the object. How do you know when you have identified them all? It is easier to answer this question when you start with a clear element of all the categories on the analytical dimension you are using. Returning to the example of analyzing a movie, if you use an analytical dimension of the plot, then there are traditional elements we should see in all plots—generating circumstance, heightening conflict/ problem, resolution, and denouement. When you have identified the specific elements the movie creators have used in their storytelling for all four components, then you can feel confident that your analysis of components is complete. If you are using an analytical dimension of major characters, there is not an easily determined number of characters that all movies have; the number varies across movies. When you are analyzing a movie by major characters, you need to decide whether the movie has one, two, five, or another number of characters that should be considered as major. If the analytical dimension you use does not come with a built-in convention for a particular number of components, then completing a **component analysis** with confidence is a bit more involved. An algorithm cannot provide you with a general rule that will always apply. If you get stuck on determining the number of components in a particular analysis, then use a heuristic for guidance (see the Identifying Number of Elements Heuristic).

If you are using a breadth approach to analyze a movie and you are using an analytical dimension of characters, then the major components would be the primary characters in the movie. If you are using an analytical dimension of plot, then the key events in the plot (generating circumstance, introduction of each problem, problem resolutions, climax, and denouement) would be the major components. If instead you are using a depth approach to analyze the movie because you are puzzled by a particular character's actions, then you would need to select another analytical dimension. Perhaps character motivations would be a useful analytical dimension in this case, and this analytical dimension might have two major categories: internal motivation and external motivation. You could elaborate this analytical dimension with subdimensions such as internal motivations (character's need to seek recognition, respect, love, or consistency) and external motivations (character is pushed into making decisions by an authority figure, fate, or pressures of time). As you use the depth approach to analyze your favorite character's motivations, you may have to elaborate your analytical dimension with additional layers of depth by adding sub-sub- or sub-sub-subdimensions. How far should an analysis go? It is impossible to give a number of levels as a general answer to this question. You need a heuristic to guide you (see the Identifying Number of Levels Heuristic). Just remember that the key to conducting a good depth approach analysis is to keep digging deeper into the message by using your creativity and logical thinking to continue developing analytical dimensions to guide you.

If you are using a combination approach to analysis, then you will need to use one analytical dimension to guide you in the identification of components in the message and a second analytical dimension to guide you in the digging down into the message. For example, let's say you are analyzing a movie and you are interested in how characters' individual motivations influence the behavior of other characters. In this situation, you would need to take a combination approach to analysis by first conducting a breadth analysis to identify all the characters, and you would then conduct a depth analysis on each of those characters in order to identify the motivations of each character. Then once you have completed these two steps, you need to look for relationships among motives and behaviors across all characters. The task in this step is rather like putting a puzzle together. You keep picking up pieces and fitting them together until all the selected pieces fit and the puzzle is completed. The puzzle pieces are the elements in the message. Conducting an analysis to determine how the authors of that message have fit all their elements together is, of course, a bit more difficult than putting a puzzle together. Pieces of a puzzle have a physical shape and color that provide clues as to how they fit together; it is often more difficult to perceive how all the pieces of a media message fit together because their clues to structure are not as concrete. However, your ability to read what these clues are will increase with practice and as your familiarity with the content of media messages grows.

When engaging in this step of analysis, your focus is on identifying how the authors have presented the elements. Be careful that you do not try to impose your own preferred elements in the analysis. Of course you can criticize the set of elements the authors have put into a message and the way they have structured those elements but that is a different task and involves the skill of evaluation more than the skill of analysis. And at times, you may be tempted to impose your own ideas about which elements should be included in the message and how those elements should be organized but again, this is a different task and involves the skills of grouping, induction, and perhaps synthesis. When applying the skill of analysis, your job is to be a recorder of other people's elements and structure instead of being a creator of another structure.

As you can see, taking a combination approach requires much more analytical work because you have to conduct an analysis with a breadth approach and then an analysis with a depth approach. This results in a lot of information about characters and their motivations, which becomes the raw material that you examine to identify relationships among characters. Because of the extra work involved in conducting a combination approach analysis, we rarely engage in such tasks. Our own motivation must be high in order to undertake such an involved task. There are times when our motivation is indeed high, such as when we are assigned such a task in a course where our work will be graded by a teacher who is testing our ability of analysis and we want to demonstrate excellence. Also, if we are in a real-world relationship that continually exhibits elements that increasingly bother us, then we have a serious problem that motivates us to work through the complexities required to analyze it with a combination approach. The combination approach is essential when we are analyzing a message for the purpose of building knowledge, because knowledge about something requires us to understand structure—that is, how elements are related to one another.

II. Heuristics

The algorithms illuminated above are the rules that are fairly generic to analysis. But the application of those algorithms might not be sufficient to complete the analysis. In partially specified problems, you will need to fill in some of the gaps on your own. To help you fill in these gaps with good decisions, four heuristics are presented below: (1) the **defining purpose heuristic**, (2) the **inductively derived positions on dimensions heuristic**, (3) the **identifying number of elements heuristic**, and (4) the **identifying number of levels heuristic**.

Heuristic 1: Defining Purpose

If you do not have a clear purpose for an analysis, you cannot complete the first step in the algorithm. When you are not sure what your purpose for the analysis should be, it is helpful to begin at Step 2 ("Determine your purpose for the analysis") and list all possible dimensions along which you could conduct the analysis. Seeing your range of options will help you focus your attention on the dimension or dimensions that seem to be most useful to you. Selecting a dimension first helps bring your purpose for the analysis to the surface.

Remember that people with well-developed knowledge structures on the topic of a message are better able to identify all possible dimensions for an analysis. But what do you do when the topic is new to you and you have no existing knowledge structure? In this case, consider that most messages lend themselves to being analyzed along the generic dimensions of structure and function. For example, let's say you want to analyze a television news program. When we think of the structure of the show, we will begin to see the component elements of a news anchor talking head, remote feed with a reporter talking at the scene, stock footage of background material, superimposed graphics, and pictures. When we break the story down functionally, we look for elements designed to inform the audience (appeals to the intellect) and elements designed to entertain the audience (appeal to emotions). Another example is an automobile. We could analyze any automobile structurally by identifying its macro sections (exterior, interior, engine) and further identifying their components. The interior is composed of the dashboard, the seats, the flooring, and so on. Automobiles can also be analyzed by their function (transportation, safety, efficiency, sex appeal, etc.).

Thinking about generic analytical dimensions is a good way to get your thinking started, but it is not a good place to stop. Once you are warmed up by thinking about generic analytical dimensions, continue to explore other dimensions that are specific to the message you want to analyze. Most messages offer other dimensions for analysis beyond the structural and functional ones. For example, a television news story can be analyzed conceptually; we could look for the elements in the story (the who, what, when, where, why, and how). A political treatise can be analyzed by type of appeal (ethos, pathos, logos). A situation comedy can be analyzed by type of humor. A series on real-life crimes can be analyzed by types of crimes portrayed and types of perpetrators. A mathematical equation can be analyzed by types of transformations (addition, subtraction, division, square roots, etc.) or branch of mathematics (trigonometry, geometry, algebra, calculus, etc.). A concert can be analyzed by types of instruments played. Fossils can be analyzed by time period. We could analyze any automobile in terms of its class (car, truck, SUV, etc.) and/or price level.

Settling on a purpose after you have assessed all of the possible dimensions for analysis has several advantages. First, this is likely to make you expand your purpose by recognizing that you can use more than one analytical dimension in your analysis. Second, you are now more confident that you have made a reasoned choice of an analytical dimension, and you are thus more likely to be committed to conducting a quality analysis.

Heuristic 2: Inductively Derived Positions on Dimensions

What do you do when you cannot identify all the neighborhoods along your analytical dimension before you begin your analysis? This is a common problem. To work your way out of this problem, you need to get started and try to identify those neighborhoods inductively as you conduct your analysis.

As an example, let's say you hear someone speak out on an issue and take a clear position. You have never heard anything about this particular issue before, but it fascinates you and you want to analyze the issue so you can understand it better. In this case, you want to use an analytical dimension that lays out all the positions people hold on the issue. Yet because the issue is brand new to you, you cannot know what all those positions are when you are planning the analysis. To avoid being stuck in this problem, work your way out of it by stating the issue in a sentence that clearly lays out a claim. Because issues are likely to be controversies, there would be at minimum one pro position and one con position. Then start reading blogs on this issue and begin categorizing bloggers as either pro (supporting the issue as you have stated it) or con (arguing against the position as you have stated it). If you notice that all pro bloggers are saying the same thing and all con bloggers are saying the same thing, then you have confirmed that there are two and only two positions on the analytical dimension. If instead you notice that there are several different kinds of pro positions, then create new categories for the pro side. You may also need to break the con side down into several different positions. You may even find that there are additional positions on this issue that are neither purely pro or purely con, which indicates a need to account for even more positions on the issue. The more you read and think about the issue, the more likely it is that you will be able to refine your analytical dimension by adding new positions, dropping others, or collapsing several inferred positions into one position.

Deriving positions inductively on an analytical dimension presents a higher degree of challenge for an analysis compared to one where the dimensions are obvious from the beginning. The need to derive positions inductively is more prevalent when you are in a new area where you do not have much prior knowledge to help you identify dimensions and positions on those dimensions before you begin the analysis. This is one reason why it is more difficult to learn about a new topic than to increase one's learning on a familiar topic. But if we fear having to engage in a larger challenge and its subsequently higher level of work required, we cannot expand our learning. So don't fall into the trap of avoiding analyses when you can't find a good analytical dimension to begin the analysis. Instead, think laterally to get out of the trap. Infer an analytical dimension. Use it as a tentative guide to position the current message. Then look for evidence of other inferred positions on that analytical dimension.

Heuristic 3: Identifying Number of Elements

How many components should be identified? This varies according to how many obvious positions there are on a given dimension and how much detail there is in the message you are analyzing. This also varies according to your conceptual differentiation ability. Those who have strong conceptual differentiation ability are likely to have many categories and subcategories compared to those who are weaker on this ability.

Instead of looking for some magic number of components as a signal to the analysis being finished, let the range and the gaps guide you. As for range, think about the scope of the analytical dimension you are using. Are you satisfied that you have examined the message for elements at both extreme ends of the analytical dimension you are using? If not, then think about the kinds of positions that would be needed to expand the scope on both ends of the analytical dimension. Also, are there gaps along the dimension you are using? If so, are there really no elements at those positions or have you missed something in the message you are analyzing? To illustrate this, use *this book* as a message and analyze it along the dimension of structural organization. Let's say we list the front matter, preface, and four chapters. This is a faulty identification of major components because it leaves out some elements such as Chapters 5 through 10, the glossary, references, and the index. Let's say instead that we list the front matter, title page, acknowledgments, preface, Chapters 1 through 10, the glossary, references, and the index. This too is faulty because the identified components are not mutually exclusive; that is, the title page and the acknowledgments are part of the front matter. While I cannot provide a magic number for how many components are needed to fill out the entire range of positions on an analytical dimension, I can suggest that your set of components is most useful when it is complete (no obvious components missing) and when the components are mutually exclusive.

Heuristic 4: Identifying Number of Levels

How far should an analysis go to display the structure the authors have used in presenting the message you are analyzing? The answer lies in your goal for the analysis. Remember, analysis is simply a tool. When you use this tool, you should have some clear purpose in mind. With a relatively simple purpose, one level of analysis may be sufficient; that is, presenting the set of major components in a message is likely to be sufficient. In this case, it may not be worth spending a great deal of effort if the importance of the message you are analyzing is low. In contrast, if you are trying to diagnose a problem that continues to bother you, then it becomes worthwhile to expend more effort and analyze the problem in more depth until its root is identified. For example, automobile mechanics who are presented with the problem of diagnosing why a car won't run will typically analyze the car beginning with the engine plant. When they break the car down into the components of interior, exterior, and engine plant, they ignore the interior and exterior—there is no need to conduct any sublevel analyses on those components. Given the purpose of the analysis, it makes sense only to conduct the analysis on the component of the engine plant. Mechanics will then focus their analysis on only the engine plant and look at each subcomponent. They would continue to rule out the subcomponents that are functioning well until they find a subcomponent that appears to be faulty. Then they will focus on only that subcomponent by examining its sub-subcomponents until eventually they track down the source of the problem. When mechanics find the irreducible unit that is faulty, they will conclude their analysis and replace that faulty unit.

III. Avoiding Traps

The path leading to the destination of a good analysis has some traps. If you get caught in one of these traps, you will not be able to reach your destination.

Many of these traps are emotional ones. When you undertake an analysis—or work with any of the other six skills—your emotions can pull you into a trap where you feel frustrated and cannot find a way out. If you can't gain control over your emotions, then you can't get out of such a trap.

You need to pay attention to your emotions and then harness them to help you, rather than allow them to become barriers preventing you from being successful. For example, if you find an analysis to be particularly difficult, let yourself get angry. Anger is a drive enhancer; it increases your heart rate and blood pressure. This translates into a greater ability to concentrate if you can prevent yourself from becoming distracted by negative feelings. Direct the energy part of your anger to forcing a breakthrough in your thinking. Don't be afraid to fight back against the dense or seemingly nonsensical information. Argue against it. Let yourself laugh out loud when something seems ridiculous. And when you have finished a particularly hard analysis, swing your arm and give your book a high five. This might sound silly, but you always want to reward yourself in some form when you are finished so that you feel good about what you have done.

Never leave a problem when you are feeling defeated by it. Instead get angry and energized. Work through the problem until you feel more positive about what you are doing, then stop at this point. You want to take your breaks when you are feeling good and successful (or at least hopeful), so that you will want to come back for more work after the break. If you take your breaks when you feel bad and defeated, you remain in the trap and it will be more difficult to get back to work. It is important to monitor your emotions so you can control them in a way that makes you more successful.

IV. Chapter Review

- It is possible, of course, to encounter a message without analyzing it. We frequently do just that. For example, we will listen to an entire song or watch an entire movie without analyzing it; that is, we could experience a message superficially as a monolithic whole. The movie is experienced as some good guys trying to stop some bad guys from committing crimes. Our unit of experience (and hence memory of it) is very superficial; that is, there is no depth of detail. There is little recognition of the many steps in the plot, no recognition of unique characters and their special contributions to the plot, and no recognition of the production elements of editing, lighting, sound, music, costuming, sets, and so forth. This is not a problem if our purpose in viewing the movie was simply to be entertained while we kill several hours. But if our purpose for watching the movie is something more (such as learning more about an issue illustrated in the movie or learning more about the crafts of acting, writing, editing, etc.), then the more we engage in analysis, the more we will learn.

- The more carefully you are able to conduct an analysis, the better will be the result, whether it is a list of components capturing the breadth of a message, a highly detailed structured outline capturing the depth of a message, or a combination of the two. This result then becomes the raw material that you will use in applying the other six skills. When you have produced a good set of mutually exclusive components (each with a detailed outline of elements revealing the authors' structures), the better you will be able to perceive the relationships among those elements, and this allows you to perform better on a variety of tasks, such as evaluation of elements, grouping of elements, induction of patterns, use of deduction, and creation of a better template for abstracting. It will also help you see gaps and problems, which puts you in a better position to conduct a high-quality synthesis.

Exercise 3.1 Practice Using the Analysis Algorithm With a Breadth Approach

1. Analyze the home page of an online newspaper.

    Object: The home page of an online newspaper

    Purpose: To determine how space is allocated in an online newspaper's home page

    Analytical Dimension: Space components

    Before beginning your analysis, list the things that you would expect to find on the home page of an online newspaper. For example, you could list things like headlines, stories, pictures, picture captions, graphics, and so forth. This list will get you started on a component analysis by helping you focus on what to look for. However, as you conduct the actual analysis, you may find other components you did not expect (refer to the Identifying Number of Elements Heuristic); add these other components to your list as you progress through your analysis.

    Identify Elements: Systematically go through the object you are analyzing (in this case, the home page of an online newspaper) and identify all components. When you have finished with one message, find another and analyze it to see if there are other components to add to your list.

    After you have analyzed several online newspapers, are you able to develop a set of components that can be used to analyze all online newspapers?

2. Again, analyze the home page of an online newspaper but this time the purpose is different, which means you need to use a different analytical dimension. Follow the guidelines provided below.

   Object: The home page of an online newspaper

   Purpose: To determine what kinds of stories are featured on the home page of an online newspaper

   Analytical Dimension: Types of stories

   Before beginning your analysis, list the types of stories you might expect to find. For example, you could list types of content in the stories, such as politics, economics, crime, accidents, disasters, and so on. Or if the online newspaper identifies itself as being based in one city, you could list story types by proximity to that city such as local stories, regional stories, national stories, and international stories.

   Identify Elements: Systematically go through the object you are analyzing (in this case, the home page of an online newspaper) and identify all components. When you have finished with one home page, find another and analyze it to see if there are other components to add to your list.

3. One more time: Analyze the home page of an online newspaper.

   Object: The home page of an online newspaper

   Purpose: To be determined by you

   Analytical Dimension: To be determined by you

   Make sure your selection of an analytical dimension is useful to fulfilling your purpose.

   Identify Elements: Systematically go through the object you are analyzing (in this case, the home page of an online newspaper) and identify all components.

4. Analyze the songs on the playlist on your mobile device, such as a smartphone, a tablet, an MP3 player, or a computer.

   Object: The set of songs on the playlist currently on your mobile device

   Purpose: To determine what kinds of songs are most prevalent in your music library

   Analytical Dimension: Genre of songs

   Some popular genres are rock, country, rap, blues, jazz, and classical. You can start with these as your initial set of components on the analytical dimension but feel free to elaborate on this set by adding, subtracting, or substituting components (refer to the Identifying Number of Elements Heuristic).

   Identify Elements: Systematically go through the object you are analyzing (in this case, the playlist of songs on your mobile device) and identify all components.

5. Analyze the songs on the playlist on your mobile device. This time choose your own purpose and analytical dimension.

(Continued)

(Continued)

Object: The set of songs on the playlist currently on your mobile device

Purpose: Your choice. Here are some suggestions for purposes you might try:

- To determine which artists are my favorites
- To determine the average age of the songs in my music library

Analytical Dimension: Your choice

Some suggested analytical dimensions you might try are artist, decade of release, and topic of the song (refer to the Inductively Derived Positions on Dimensions Heuristic).

Identify Elements: Systematically go through the object you are analyzing (in this case, the playlist of songs on your mobile device) and identify all components.

Exercise 3.2 Practice Using the Analysis Algorithm With a Combination Approach

1. Analyze a chapter in a textbook; limit your analysis to one section in one chapter.

   Object: One chapter in a textbook

   Purpose: To identify how many facts are presented on a particular topic

   Analytical Dimension: Use an analytical dimension that includes the components of facts, transition sentences (introductions, summaries etc.), authors' opinions, and examples (refer to the Identifying Number of Elements Heuristic and the Inductively Derived Positions on Dimensions Heuristic).

   Identify Elements: Focus your attention on the object you are analyzing for depth (in this case, the one section of a chapter in the textbook) and identify the elements that fit into each of the areas on the analytical dimension (components and layers within each component).

2. Analyze a chapter in a textbook.

   Object: One chapter in a textbook

   Purpose: Your choice (refer to the Identifying Number of Levels Heuristic)

   Analytical Dimension: The challenge in this exercise is to think up the dimensions yourself. If this is an introductory-level textbook by a mainstream American publisher, it is likely that the structure is presented very clearly with layout conventions, typefaces, font sizes, color, and so on (refer to the Identifying Number of Elements Heuristic and the Inductively Derived Positions on Dimensions Heuristic).

Levels: Allow the message to determine how many levels you will use. However, to make this exercise meaningful, go down at least two levels; to make this exercise manageable, do not go down more than four levels.

Identify Elements: Systematically scan through the object of your combination analysis (in this case the chapter) to identify all components and groups of components.

3. Analyze a newspaper article. Choose an article that is at least five or six paragraphs long so it presents enough detail for a challenging analysis.

Object: Newspaper article

Purpose: To determine the structure of information in the article

Analytical Dimension: The challenge in this exercise is to think up the dimensions for yourself.

Levels: Allow the message to determine how many levels you will use. However, to make this exercise meaningful, go down at least two levels; to make this exercise manageable, do not go down more than four levels.

ntify Elements: Systematically scan through the object of your ation analysis (in this case, the article) to identify all components and components.

ding in which a college class is held.

e how space is used in the building

s of space usage

list the types of usages of space that you
you could list classrooms, bathrooms,
he outline analysis, you also need to
nized into groups. For example,
aces and private spaces, or you
deciding on which grouping
alysis and what would be
the purpose statement
help in guiding
bout who might
marshal, the
erson with
ise the
e more

identify all
ished with one
there are other
ll components you

Evaluating

Making Judgments About the Value of Media Messages

Evaluation is making an assessment of the worth of an element. This process of assessing the value of something basically requires the comparing of an element to a **standard**. If you judge that the element meets your standard, then you conclude that the element is acceptable or okay. If you judge that the element falls short of your standard, then you conclude that the element is unacceptable. And if you judge that the element exceeds your standard, then you conclude that the element is excellent (or some positive synonym) because it has not only met but also exceeded the standard.

The two essential parts of any evaluation are a standard and an element. Standards are the benchmarks we use when judging the value of elements. The elements are particular characteristics (such as facts, advertising claims, story plot points, characters, etc.) that we identified in objects, especially in media messages, that were generated through the use of the skill of analysis. Therefore, we must do an analysis first before we are able to do an evaluation.

Standards are our beliefs about how things should be. Oftentimes the judgments we make about elements tell us more about our standards than about the elements we are evaluating.

It is possible, of course, to encounter a message without evaluating it, but then we have no option but to accept the message as is without making a judgment about its value. For example, you can read an entire magazine article without ever considering its value to you. You simply acquire facts as you read through the magazine article and never ask yourself questions about whether those facts will have value to you. Instead you simply assume that the information you are acquiring will be useful to you later in discussions or in making decisions. You also are likely to be assuming that all the information presented in the article is accurate and unbiased.

Evaluating requires a skeptical attitude that elements might not always be valuable to us for various reasons, such as their utility or accuracy. This skepticism is often referred to as "critical viewing" (Messaris, 1994), "critical thinking" (Brown, 1991), or just "critical" (McLaren, Hammer, Sholle, & Reilly, 1995; Silverblatt, 1995). When people talk about a "critical analysis," they usually mean an "evaluation," because they seem to be alluding to a process where media messages are challenged as not being up to some standard.

There is a lot of evidence showing that people simply accept the opinions they hear in media messages without making their own evaluations. One example of this is the now widespread opinion that the U.S. educational

...ally than a child who watches a moderate amoun... week). Thus, the pattern is as follows: Children who ...of information that television provides do less well in sch... ...watch a moderate amount of television; however, when a chil... ...nt where the amount of television viewing cuts into needed study ...performance goes down. Television, as well as the Internet and ...f media, has potentially positive as well as negative effects. ...re can displace constructive behaviors such as studying; but ...and our experience, teach us valuable social lessons, and ...nations. Preventing children from watching television can ...negative effect but it prevents positive effects as well.

...e question "What effect does viewing television have ...: performance?" we could give the simple, popular ...nded. It is also misleading because it reinforces the ...ative effect. But now you can see that this answer is ...fects are negative and that the media are to blame. ...s are such a dangerous trap is because they are ...n that as people are continually exposed to faulty ...ed to challenge them. When someone points ...re secure that their faulty beliefs are accurate. ...h their beliefs are based is faulty, they do not ...y are so sure that they are correct. Thus, over ...examine their beliefs, but they are also less ...s other than their own are correct.

...evaluation (Table 4.1). Although ...r times you may find yourself ...own order so that you ca... ...r, it is best to proce... ...hen to deviate wh...

...nat ...ss well

academi...
hours per
the source
children wh...
gets to the po...
time, academi...
all other forms...
Television expos...
television can exp...
stimulate our imag...
prevent a potentially...
When we pose t...
on a child's academi...
answer: There is a neg...
too simple—it is simplem...
limited belief that media e...
The reason faulty belie...
self-reinforcing. By this, I me...
information, they feel even m...
They feel less and less motiva...
out that the information on whi...
accept this criticism because the...
time, they are not only less likely to...
tolerant of the possibility that belief...

CH...
...stem is not very good and a big reason...
...too much time with the media, especi...
National Center for Education Statisti...
standardized testing to assess the...
ing, science, and mathematics...
levels of learning with those of...
for International Student A...
United States are ranked...
ematics (National Cen...
educational system...
too much time wi...
creativity, and t...
children will...
This c...
is that it...
perfo...
for...

I. The Evaluation Algorith...

There are five steps in applying t...
the steps are presented in a singl...
going back to repeat steps and t...
meet the demands of a particula...
through the steps in the follow...
you have a good reason to do s...

Step 1: Select Elements

The need to employ the s...
encounter an element that...
...in us. For example, you se...

TABLE 4.1   The Skill of Evaluating

Purpose: To assess the worth of an element

Pre-Task: Conduct an analysis to identify focal elements in the message.

Algorithm:

1. Select elements.

2. Select a standard for the evaluation.

3. Determine the most appropriate criteria set(s) for each standard.

4. Compare an element to each criterion in the criteria set and make a judgment about whether:

    a. the element matches the criterion (acceptable),

    b. the element exceeds the criterion (excel), or

    c. the element falls short of the criterion (failure).

5. Construct a summary judgment about the value of the element.

    a. If the element receives a uniform judgment on all criteria, then the summary judgment is the same as any one of the judgments on the individual criteria.

    b. If the element does not receive a uniform judgment on all criteria, then weight the criteria in terms of relative importance and use your judgments on the weightiest criteria to influence most the construction of your summary judgment.

feel must be exaggerated. This motivates you to evaluate that claim (the element) for accuracy (the standard). Or you see a news report on your smartphone and the reporter presents a fact attributed to a source that you never heard of before, which makes you wonder if the source is unbiased. This motivates you to evaluate the source (the element) of the fact for bias (the standard). Or you start watching a video for a series you have never seen before; after a few minutes of viewing, you start to like the show but you wonder if it will be good enough to continue watching. This motivates you to start engaging in an ongoing evaluation of all kinds of elements in the show (characters, plot points, settings, music, etc.) and continuously compare those unfolding elements to your personal standard for what is acceptable entertainment for you.

In each of the three examples presented above, the elements arose naturally out of an experience with a media message. It is a common occurrence for elements to present themselves in a way that stimulates our use of the skill of evaluation. But there are also other ways that we identify elements that will create a need for us to use this skill. For example, let's say you are assigned to write a term paper on a particular topic for a class. The topic guides you to expose yourself to particular media messages (such as books, journals, and websites) to get information. As you read through the information you encounter, you are constantly looking for relevant facts. Thus the facts you encounter are the elements and your standard in this continuing process of evaluation is relevancy; that is, does each fact meet your standard of being relevant to the topic of the term paper?

As you can see from all of these examples, we need to identify elements in order to conduct an evaluation, and the identification of those elements requires the use of the skill of analysis. There are times when those elements present themselves to us in such a natural way that it might seem we are not using our skill of analysis but we still are engaging in analysis. There are other times when it is much more obvious that we are using the skill of analysis to identify elements. These examples also illustrate that the elements we use in an evaluation can be singular or multiple. A single element is enough to trigger an evaluation, but evaluations can also be ongoing when we start considering a flow of multiple elements.

Step 2: Select a Standard

The second step in using the skill of evaluation is to select a standard to use in assessing the value of an element. Oftentimes we select a standard without much thought, or we use a standard purely out of habit. But when the evaluation task is an important one, it is better to spend some effort to consider your range of options for a standard.

With media literacy, there are generally four domains of standards: cognitive, emotional, moral, and aesthetic. **Cognitive standards** are the benchmarks that make something satisfying to the mind, such as accuracy. Accuracy is a common standard. You can compare an element to what you already know about a topic. If the new element does not fit with what you already know, then you would judge the new element to be inaccurate. The problem with this is that perhaps your standard for accuracy is faulty. Therefore, it is usually better to try to use an external standard for accuracy rather than always relying on your internalized standards for accuracy (see section III on avoiding traps).

Another cognitive type of standard is utility. The standard of utility requires an understanding of your existing knowledge structures. The way your knowledge is arranged will tell you if you need the new element that you are evaluating. You ask yourself if this new element is something you would find useful to incorporate into your existing knowledge structures. Utility comes in three forms. One form is to extend your knowledge structure by adding a new element on a new topic, thus broadening your knowledge structure. Another form is to add an element to an existing knowledge topic to extend its depth. A third way is to add another example to a fact you already have in your knowledge structure. This adds weight to that point. The third way is the easiest to achieve because it is the least threatening to existing knowledge structures. We know from years of research on information processing that humans like to add new elements to what they already believe because this avoids cognitive dissonance.

In addition to cognitive standards, there are **emotional standards**, which are expectations that a message should evoke a particular emotional reaction in the person. For example, people often go to horror films in order to feel fear to a higher degree than they have ever felt before. The expectation for a certain level of fear is the standard; videos that do not deliver the intensity of fear that audience members expect are regarded as disappointing.

Moral standards are the benchmarks that make something satisfying to a person's code of ethics or religion. Many people are offended by elements in the media (such as violence, sex, and "bad" language) because these elements fall egregiously below their moral standards.

Moral evaluations of media message elements can trigger emotions, such as offense, anger, or outrage when people judge those elements to fall below their moral standards. In contrast, when elements exceed an individual's moral standards, they can trigger more positive emotions such as satisfaction, happiness, and admiration.

Aesthetic standards are the benchmarks people use to judge the artistic quality of a message. For example, when we evaluate a video, we can focus on the artistic ability evidenced by the actors, directors, writers, music composers, editors, costumers, lighting crew, editors, and so on. The more experience we have watching videos, and especially in engaging in the crafts required to produce videos, the more elaborate our aesthetic standards will be. This is why experienced video critics are often harder to please. Because they have a great deal of knowledge about good and bad videos, a video has to exceed standards on many criteria in order to be considered good.

Because most evaluations are not simple one-dimensional tasks, we need to realize that there are multiple standards that could be used simultaneously to evaluate a particular message. When we evaluate a video, we don't usually begin with a summary judgment. Instead, we have a set of standards we use. For example, when we evaluate a video, some people focus on characters and plot exclusively. They have a standard for characters and one for plot, so if a video features their favorite stars and has a strong but typically Hollywood movie type of story, they will conclude that the video was good. Someone else who sees the same video and has a different set of criteria (moral theme and off-beat plot) may judge the video to be bad. The judgment of value follows from the standards, so it is important that you are aware of your standards when you begin an evaluation.

Knowledge structures are very important to the process of evaluation because they contain information that forms standards. For example, let's say you make a new friend and later go to her Facebook page to get more information about her. If this is the first time you have ever accessed a Facebook page, your knowledge structure about Facebook is almost blank and thus you have no information to give your expectations. In contrast, if you have accessed hundreds of Facebook pages and have constructed your own page, then you have a good deal of information to set your expectations.

Step 3: Determine Criteria for Standards

Criteria are the conditions that must be met to achieve the standard. Unless these can be written clearly and with detail, the standard itself may not be useful. For example, let's say you listen to a popular song and you judge it to be "cool." This judgment implies an evaluation on the standard of coolness and this song exceeded your minimum criteria for being cool. This judgment may be fine for you, especially if you regard cool as an emotional standard and you look for things that trigger that feeling of cool in you. But if you had to explain your evaluation to someone else, it would be difficult because you probably haven't articulated the criteria of coolness. If you were assigned to evaluate the song for a music appreciation class or to write a music column for a newspaper, you would need to say something more beyond, "This is a cool song." You would need to articulate your criteria for coolness and explain in detail what characteristics a song would have to exhibit in order for the song to be judged as "cool."

Consider another example such as the evaluation of student performance in courses. Typically, student performance is judged with labels such as excellent (A), good (B), average (C), poor (D), or failing (F). But rarely do teachers evaluate student work by providing only a letter grade. Students want an explanation about how teachers evaluated their work to be a particular letter; that is, they want to know what the standards were. When teachers explain their standards, they are giving students detail about how the students can meet or exceed those standards.

Almost all standards appear on the surface to be categorical, but most are really based on an implied continuum. Let's return to the example of course grades. The five letters used for grades are categories of performance, but they are not natural categories; instead, they are derived from a continuum of performance that ranges from zero (no performance) to 100% (perfect performance). Typically if your performance reaches or exceeds a criterion of 90%, your performance is given the label of excellent. Excellence in this example is not a category in the sense that being a male or a female are categories.

When an evaluation is important, you need to think carefully about whether your standard is a set of categories or a continuum. If it is a set of categories, you need to specify criteria for what is required to be included in each category. If instead your standard relies on a continuum, you need to decide two things when establishing your criteria. First, you need to think about how to position the elements on the continuum; that is, what characteristics need to be present in the element to move it up (or down) on the continuum? Second, you need to decide how to label the neighborhoods on the continuum. In the simplest case, you need to label two neighborhoods:

acceptable and nonacceptable. At what point on the continuum do you draw the line of acceptability? Returning again to our course grading example above, how should you draw the lines between grades? Should 90% and 99% both be labeled as an A? Or should a 90% be an A−? Or should 90% perhaps be a B+ or even a B? Making these decisions is difficult, but this needs to be done. You need to set the criteria clearly.

Step 4: Compare Elements to the Criteria on the Standard

The fourth step is to compare an element to each criterion in the standard and make a judgment about whether (a) the element matches the criterion and is therefore acceptable, (b) the element exceeds the standard and is therefore judged as excelling, or (c) the element falls short of the criterion and is therefore judged as falling short. The simplest type of evaluation to make is one where your purpose is clear, the standard is clear and simple, and the judgment is a simple categorical one.

Step 5: Construct a Summary Judgment

This step is required when you have multiple criteria. Of course if the element exceeds each criterion, then it is a simple matter to conclude overall that the element excels. Or if the element falls short of each criterion, then it is also simple to conclude that the element fails. Thus if the element receives a uniform judgment on all criteria, then the summary judgment is the same as any one of the judgments on the individual criteria.

What do you do when the element exceeds some criteria and falls short on others (that is, when the pattern is mixed)? This presents a more difficult challenge, a challenge that you are likely to confront frequently. For example, your friend asks you for your evaluation of a video you just saw and she wants to know if she should see it or not. Thus your recommendation must be based on multiple criteria but it needs to be delivered as a category—that is, either yes or no. Let's say you evaluated the performance of the lead actress to be outstanding but the directing and writing were poor. So the video excels on one criterion but fails on two other criteria. On balance, do you recommend the video (yes) or not (no)? If you regard all three criteria to be equally important in determining your recommendation, then you will conclude with a negative recommendation.

II. Heuristics

In the evaluation process presented above, there are at least two places where the demands of your evaluation task will lead you to believe the task is only partially specified. In those instances you need to exert your own judgment to generate more guidance for yourself and thereby more fully specify the task. As we discuss below, the **category constructing heuristic** and the **multiple elements heuristic** will help guide you in exercising this judgment.

Heuristic 1: Constructing Categories

When dealing with continua, there is always the problem of drawing the lines to create categories. How do you draw these lines in a way that does not seem arbitrary or unfair? To illustrate this problem, let's say you are interested in how the news covers political candidates running for office. The unit of interest to you is the sound bite, where the candidate is shown onscreen speaking about his or her position on some issue. You have analyzed 10 news videos and identified 25 sound bites of political candidates. You have measured the length of each sound bite and they range from 3 seconds to 90 seconds. You want to make an evaluative judgment about how well the news covers candidates' positions, as indicated by how much time they show candidates speaking in their own words. What standard do you use? How do you determine what is the acceptable length of a sound bite? Are you willing to say that a sound bite of 20 seconds is long enough to present the candidate but anything shorter than that is too superficial?

There are three techniques you can consider using in order to make your line-drawing seem less arbitrary. First, you could use the same criteria and lines as someone else who has worked on a similar evaluation. The danger here is that the other person may have constructed the criteria poorly, so your use of that weak design will result in a questionable evaluation. In order to avoid perpetuating other people's mistakes, think about whether their criteria seem any less arbitrary and any more meaningful than criteria that you could develop on your own.

A second technique is to find some credible benchmark outside of the evaluation process that could be brought into that process as a way of justifying the drawing of a line in a particular place. With the sound bite example, perhaps you could find a research study explains that when people are exposed to factual information in messages longer than 30 seconds, their understanding and recall is dramatically better. If you could find such a research study, then you have a good reason to draw your line of acceptability at 30 seconds.

A third technique you can use to make your line-drawing less arbitrary is to avoid drawing those lines before you look at the distribution of elements on the standard's continuum. Instead, look at the distribution and notice where the clusters of elements are. With the example of student performance in courses, faculty often plot the performance of all students in a class and look at the distribution before deciding where to draw the line between an A and a B, and so on. Let's say in a class of 25 students, the highest performance was by a student who earned 93% and there was a cluster of eight students between 88% and 93% and another cluster of 10 students between 77% and 81%. In this case, it would *not* be good to draw the line between an A and a B at 90% because there is little difference between the performances of the eight students in the 5-point cluster from 88% to 93%; they all excelled relative to the rest of the students in the class, and all should get A's. This group scored significantly higher than the 10 students clustered in the 4-point range of 77% to 81%, so these 10 students should all receive the same grade but a step lower (a B) than the group of eight students in the top cluster. Thus the line between an A and a B should be drawn around 85%.

Heuristic 2: Multiple Elements

The simplest form of evaluation is to use a standard composed of only one criterion. However, oftentimes it makes more sense to take more than one criterion into consideration simultaneously. For example, let's say you wanted to evaluate American universities and find the best one for you. Let's say you wanted to major in journalism. You select a standard of "journalism program." Either a school offers a major in journalism (meets standard and is therefore acceptable) or it does not (unacceptable). It is relatively easy to evaluate the utility of each university in being able to meet this simple standard that is composed of only one criterion. But let's say you end up with 80 universities that meet this simple standard; that is, you have found 80 universities that have journalism programs. This group of 80 offers too many examples, so you decide to get more sophisticated in your evaluation. You elaborate your standard by considering multiple criteria. Let's say you create a standard with four criteria as follows: number of journalism courses offered (the more the better), number of internship opportunities (the more the better), the quality of internship opportunities (the more prestigious the news organization the better), and the reputation of the faculty (the more Pulitzer prizes won the better). You want to consider all of these factors, so you must use a **standard-complex**.

There are two major challenges of using a standard-complex. One challenge is with determining which elements should be included in the standard-complex. In the above example, it is obvious that there are many ways of evaluating the quality of a journalism program. The example above included four criteria but there are many others that we could have included.

The second challenge of using a standard-complex is making a summary judgment when using multiple criteria. Should all criteria be weighted equally in making the summary judgment? In our journalism example, should each of the four criteria contribute the same to the overall evaluation? Maybe one is much more important than the others and should be given a heavier weight in determining the overall evaluation. For example, perhaps a program has few courses on the books and not many listed internship possibilities, but there is one faculty member there who has won three Pulitzer prizes and she is an excellent mentor. In this case, the one criterion of quality of one faculty member can be strong enough to compensate for shortcomings in all other areas so that your summary judgment is that the journalism program exceeds your standard.

Like with all heuristics, I cannot prescribe which is best for you. But by providing you with the guidelines in this chapter, I have alerted you to the key things you need to think about when making your own decisions.

III. Avoiding Traps

The application of the skill of evaluation is basically a simple one if you are organized and systematic. However, there are some traps. I point out six of these traps below.

Trap 1: Too Limited a Standard

It is important to start serious evaluations with a careful consideration of all possible standards. If you intuitively select a standard for the sake of convenience, your evaluation will likely have little use. It is better to explore all relevant standards across the different types—cognitive, moral, emotional, and aesthetic. It is also wise to incorporate multiple criteria in the standard. This makes the evaluation more complex to work through, but the results will usually be more valuable.

Trap 2: Too Trusting of Existing Beliefs

Our standards typically come from our beliefs. We all have beliefs about what makes someone attractive, successful, witty, entertaining, trustworthy, smart, and on and on. While our existing beliefs are essential for determining our standards that we use in evaluations, those beliefs should not automatically be trusted for accuracy or usefulness. For example, people who have strongly held beliefs on controversial issues will typically avoid information counter to their beliefs and give extra weight to information that supports their beliefs. Over time, some beliefs become faulty as the information that has supported those beliefs is found to be faulty or out of date, yet many people still hold onto those discredited beliefs. This is why media literacy emphasizes an open mind, so people are willing to continually seek out new information and update their beliefs when the balance of information supporting or refuting those beliefs shifts. As an example, let's say you hear a very damaging claim against a political candidate that you favor. Your existing knowledge structure is composed of a large number of positive elements about this candidate, so your belief about the candidate is very positive. The new claim does not fit into your existing knowledge structure, so you must decide whether to believe the new claim and incorporate it into your knowledge base, which would require substantial alterations, or to disregard the new claim. There are several techniques you could use to work through this task. You could use an accuracy standard and examine the credibility of the claim; that is, who is the source of the accusation and does it seem plausible? Another technique is a weighting one. If the claim sits out there by itself with no additional people coming forth to support it, then the claim has little weight, especially compared to the weight of favorable knowledge you already have about the candidate.

If we disregard all information that does not conform to our already existing beliefs, then we will have no chance of altering those beliefs as the world changes. We become out of date and irrelevant by holding anachronistic beliefs based on now faulty information. Some people want to protect their old beliefs and perspectives at any costs. Preserving traditions and being loyal are important, so there is something to be said for screening out new information. But when all discrepant new information is screened out purely for the sake of convenience or to avoid minor emotional frustrations, then people lose the ability to process all information that does not reinforce their narrowing existence.

Trap 3: Credibility of the Source

Another trap is comparing the message element to the standard without taking into consideration the source of the message. Not all media vehicles are equally credible, so the information they provide varies across sources. When you find information from a source that employs professional journalists and has a long tradition of accuracy, you can trust that information much more than when you find information from publications such as the *National Enquirer.*

It is also important to be careful in evaluating information presented by people who are labeled as experts. There is a halo effect with messages from experts; that is, we have been conditioned to believe that we should trust and believe experts. Remember that even the best experts are sometimes wrong because of faulty reasoning. Ask yourself: What makes this person an expert? Being an expert is not a categorical position; it is continuous. Some experts are more expert than are others. And in some areas such as weather and the economy, all experts are wrong much of the time. We should analyze their claims to see if this is one of the times they are right before we accept what they say as fact.

Another facet of evaluating the source of information is to examine how the information was generated. A prime example of this is the public opinion survey. If we accept the findings reported in the press and allow journalists to affect our beliefs, we can often be misled. We need to inquire into the reputation of the surveyor, the nature of the sample (who was asked the questions), and especially the wording of the questions. For example, let's say we hear that the president's approval rating has climbed to 70%. That sounds pretty good. But what does it really mean? Does this mean that the approval is high but only among people who answered their telephone the evening the poll was taken? Or only among people living in cities? We need to know something about the sample. We also need to know what approval is based on. Does this mean approval of handling the office in terms of domestic issues, foreign policy, or both? Or does it mean that the president hasn't done anything to screw up the economy (i.e., he is good at staying out of the way and doing nothing)? Or does it mean that people simply like him as a moral human being? And we need to know how the question was asked. Although the following three questions could be used to measure approval of the president, people are likely to provide different answers to each of these questions: (1) Do you think the president is doing an excellent job? (2) Do you think the president is doing a satisfactory job? (3) Do you think the president is doing the best job he can, given his limitations? Finally, we need to know what answer choices were available to the respondents in the public opinion poll. Did the pollsters give people only two choices (yes or no), did they factor in the possibility that many people may not have an opinion (yes, no, or no opinion), and did they measure degree of support (doing a great job, doing a good job, doing an okay job, or doing a bad job)? All of these factors in the sampling, the pollster's idea of "good job," the wording of the questions, and the answer choices have a significant influence on shaping the results of public opinion polls. People who simply accept the reported results of public opinion polls without analyzing the key factors that generated those results are in danger of being misled.

Trap 4: Evaluating Percentages

Oftentimes you will find a fact (in a focal plan analysis) that is a percentage. These numbers can be especially troublesome because they look simple, but they can be very misleading. The trap is that many percentages are not literally inaccurate; instead accurate percentages can be misleading when people do not understand how those percentages were computed. Remember that percentages are computed from fractions where one number (the numerator on the top of the fraction) is compared to another number (the denominator on the bottom of the fraction). When the denominator matches the context of the situation, then the percentage is an accurate fact for that situation. However, people often take a percentage used in one situation and use it to make a case in a different situation. In these cases, you need to check to see if the denominator has been changed to reflect the change in situation. To illustrate, let's consider an example of an argument that the divorce rate is now 50% in this country. This figure is a percentage, and like all percentages, it is computed from two numbers. What are those numbers? If we compare the number of marriages with the number of divorces in any given year, we get a ratio of 2 to 1. In other words there were twice as many marriages last year as there were divorces, or expressed another way, the number of divorces last year was 50% of the number of marriages. But this makes it sound like half the married people get divorced each year, and this surface interpretation is wrong. If we change the base number of the comparison, we get a very different number. Let's compare the number of divorces last year with the number of total *existing* marriages at the beginning of that year.

When we make this comparison, we get a figure of about 1%. This means that last year, 1% of all existing marriages ended in divorce by the end of that year. Which is the correct divorce rate: 50% or 1%? They both are. The difference is attributable to a difference in the base of comparison, where both bases of comparison are legitimate. Because the bases are different, they are answering different questions. If the question is "What percentage of existing marriages will end in divorce this year?" the answer is 1%. But if the question is "What is the ratio of the number of marriages this year to the number of divorces this year?" then the answer is 50%.

See how percentages can be misleading? It is important that you always evaluate the credibility of the numbers—especially percentages—that the media present. If you do not do this, you are in danger of interpreting the wrong meaning even when the figures are accurate. Sometimes you will not be able to find all the information you need in an analysis of a message making a particular claim (that is, the author did not provide enough detail). In this case you need to go to other messages the author quotes and conduct your analysis on the author's primary sources.

Trap 5: Analyzing Claims for Causal Relationships

Sometimes an argument in a media message will be based on causal claims. A causal claim is something like this: A causes B, so when we have an A, a B will always follow; and when we have a B, there is an A preceding it. It is natural for people to observe happenings and then seek explanations for why those happenings occurred. But sometimes the reasoning is wrong because of one or more fallacies. One of these is the *ecological fallacy*, where an argument claims that there is a causal relationship between two things merely because they occur together. For example, in the 1950s it was found that crime rates were the highest in neighborhoods where immigrants were most numerous. Some people used this "co-occurrence" to argue that immigrants were a cause of crime. But a careful analysis of this situation revealed that immigrants were forced to live in neighborhoods where crime rates were already high; they could not afford more expensive housing in safer neighborhoods. Immigrants themselves committed very few of the crimes (Strauss, 1996). Unless you analyze the claim carefully, you would misinterpret the relationship and thereby construct a faulty belief.

Another problem with a causal claim is what I call the *butterfly fallacy*. This is named after the belief that if a butterfly flaps its wings today in the Amazon basin, it will trigger a chain of events that will eventually lead to rain in your hometown next week. The problem with this "connection" is that there are too many influences occurring simultaneously, any one of which could account for the rain. You would need to evaluate the viability of each link in the very long causal chain from the Amazon to your house in order to see if there were any faulty links that would invalidate the jumping from a particular cause to a far-removed effect.

Be careful of relative words, such as *best*, *largest*, *fastest*, *cheapest*, and so on. These words need to be analyzed to see what is really being compared. For example, economists continually are developing sophisticated mathematical models to predict facets of the stock market or the economy. Some of these models are better than others at predicting the performance of certain stocks; however, be careful to understand that better is not perfection. My predictive model may be better than any of the others, because I am right 35% of the time, while everyone else is right only 20% of the time. If you invest with me, it will be better than using other models, but you will still lose money most of the time.

Trap 6: Avoid Being Defeated by Weak Natural Abilities

To conduct a good evaluation, one must avoid being impulsive and being locked into vertical thinking. Also, we need the product of a good analysis, which relies on field independency and conceptual differentiation. Many of us are relatively weak on one of more of these abilities. If we let our weaknesses stop us from conducting serious, systematic, multifaceted evaluations, we will not be able to make good judgments, nor will we be able to get better at this skill of evaluation. People who have more highly developed evaluation skills will be more careful, reasonable, diligent, and logical when making evaluative judgments. People with lesser developed evaluation skills will feel the effort is not worth it and quickly make a judgment based only on superficial intuition.

The more information a person already has, the easier it is to make judgments about new information. For example, if people use a knowledge structure with only cognitive information, they have the basis for undertaking a logical reasoning process. But what happens when this logical process results in several good judgment alternatives? Had we also had some emotional information in that knowledge structure, we could draw on that additional knowledge. Goleman (1995) reminds us that an important part of evaluation is emotions. Unless we factor in how we feel about something, we may become paralyzed and not be able to make a judgment. We need to have enough self-awareness about our emotions to determine where our preferences lie. Goleman says that many decisions "cannot be made well through sheer rationality; they require gut feeling, and the emotional wisdom garnered through past experiences" (p. 53).

IV. Chapter Review

- If we encounter a message without evaluating it, we allow it to pass through our filter untested. Thus, faulty and useless information passes through along with the accurate and important, without us knowing which is which. It is therefore important to judge the elements in the flow of information against some standard. The more carefully you are able to conduct an evaluation, the higher quality your judgments will be.

- A good evaluation relies on two things: (1) selection of a good standard and (2) the systematic comparison of an element with the standard. A good standard is one that is selected after a full consideration of all the options, including cognitive, moral, emotional, and aesthetic components. The standard should have clear criteria to guide your judgments on the elements.

- Unless evaluation is to be superficial, it must begin with an analysis of the message and produce a good set of elements. The elements should be tested for source credibility then weighted accordingly.

Exercise 4.1 Practice Using the Evaluation Algorithm

This exercise is a sequence of five challenges designed to increase your understanding of using your skill of evaluation. This sequence starts with the easiest challenges by providing you with the maximum degree of guidance. As you progress through this sequence, you will find the exercises increasingly challenging because you will have to do more of the thinking for yourself.

Challenge I

Find a source of jokes (e.g., a book, CD, website, etc.). The task is to evaluate a joke on a dichotomous standard of humorousness.

1. *Select an Element:* Pick one joke that you have not heard before.

2. *Select a Standard:* Use the standard of humorousness. This will be a simple, dichotomous standard. Either the joke is humorous or it is NOT humorous.

3. *Determine the Most Appropriate Criterion:* In this exercise, the criterion for "humorousness" is whether the joke makes you laugh or not.

4. *Compare the Element to the Standard:* Read (or listen to) the selected joke and observe whether you laugh or not. If you DID laugh, judge the joke to be humorous; if you did NOT laugh, judge the joke to fail to be humorous.

Challenge II

Find a source of jokes (e.g., a book, a CD, a website, etc.). The task is to evaluate a joke on a continuous standard of humorousness.

1. *Select an Element:* Pick one joke that you have not heard before.

2. *Select a Standard:* Use the standard of humorousness. This will be a continuous standard, so it will not be a simple two category decision of finding the joke either humorous or not humorous. Instead the standard should have multiple thresholds, so that it can be judged as terrible, not funny, a little funny, funny, or hilarious.

(Continued)

(Continued)

3. *Determine the Most Appropriate Criterion:* In this exercise, we need five criteria to tell us which of the five levels of "humorousness" the joke should be judged as. Use these criteria:

   • Terrible—joke elicits groans and moans

   • Not funny—joke elicits no reaction

   • A little funny—joke elicits a smile

   • Funny—joke elicits a laugh

   • Hilarious—joke elicits uncontrollable and even painful laughter

4. *Compare the Element to the Standard:* Read (or listen to) the selected joke and observe which of the five reactions (the criteria) you exhibit.

Challenge III

Find a source of songs. The task is to evaluate a song on a *dichotomous* standard of good.

1. *Select the Element:* Pick one song that you have not heard before.

2. *Select a Standard:* Use a *dichotomous* standard of good. You will make a judgment about whether this song is good or not.

3. *Determine the Most Appropriate Criterion:* Define "good song." This will be a personal criterion; what you regard as a good song is likely to be different than what other people regard as a good song. That is okay. The challenge here is not to try to come up with the ultimate definition of "good song" that everyone will accept; instead the challenge is for you to articulate your own personal criteria for "good song" in as much detail as you can.

   • Think about cognitive criteria, such as who the artist is, what the genre is, what instruments are used, the year it was released, and so on.

   • Think about emotional criteria, such as how the song makes you feel.

   • Think about moral criteria, such as whether the song deals with an ethical issue and if so, what position it takes on the issue.

   • Think about aesthetic criteria, such as how skilled was the lyricist, the musicians, the sound mixing, the editing, and so forth.

4. *Compare the Element to the Standard:* Listen to the song and observe your reaction to it. If the song meets all your criteria, then you will evaluate it as being good. If it meets none of your criteria, then you will evaluate it as NOT being good. What if the song meets some but not all of your criteria?

Challenge IV

Find a source of songs. The task is to evaluate a song on a *continuous* standard of good.

1. *Select an Element:* Pick one song that you have not heard before.

2. *Select a Standard:* Use a *continuous* standard of good. You will make a judgment about the degree to which the song is good or bad. Think about

how many degrees you want to build into your standard, then assign a label to each of the degrees. For example, your standard may use five degrees for a song, such as terrible, weak, okay, good, and super-good.

3. *Determine the Most Appropriate Criteria:* For each of the degrees on our standard, you need to write a list of criteria that would guide you in determining which degree best shows your judgment of the song's relative degree of "goodness." As with the previous exercise, think about cognitive, emotional, moral, and aesthetic criteria.

4. *Compare the Element to the Standard:* Listen to the song and observe your reaction to it on each criterion. If the song meets all of your criteria, then you will likely evaluate it as having the highest degree on your "goodness" continuum. And if the song meets none of your criteria, then you will likely evaluate it as the lowest degree on your "goodness" continuum. When you do not have a simple, all-or-nothing pattern (how many times the element meets criteria), then look for the place on the standard's continuum where the element met most of the criteria and this is your evaluation judgment.

Challenge V

Find a source of songs. The task is to evaluate a song on a continuous standard of good.

1. *Select an Element:* Pick one song that you have not heard before.

2. *Select a Standard:* Use a continuous standard of good. You will make a judgment about the degree to which the song is good or bad. Think about how many degrees you want to build into your standard, then assign a label to each of the degrees. For example, your standard may use five degrees for a song, such as terrible, weak, okay, good, and super-good.

3. *Determine the Most Appropriate Criteria:* For each of the degrees on our standard, you need to write a list of criteria that would guide you in determining which degree best shows your judgment of the song's relative degree of "goodness." As with the previous exercise, think about cognitive, emotional, moral, and aesthetic criteria.

4. *Compare the Element to the Standard:* Listen to the song and observe your reaction to it on each criterion. If the song meets all of your criteria, then you will likely evaluate it as having the highest degree on your "goodness" continuum. And if the song meets none of your criteria, then you will likely evaluate it as the lowest degree on your "goodness" continuum. But more typically, the song will not meet either all or none of your criteria, and this sets up a challenge that you need to undertake in the next step.

5. *Construct a Summary Judgment:* In constructing your summary judgment, you have two challenges: weighting and thresholds.

   • As for weighting, think about all the criteria you have. If you believe that each criterion is equally important, then you could simply sum up all the times a song met each criterion and use that to guide your summary judgment. But more typically you are likely to regard some criteria as

(Continued)

(Continued)

more important than other criteria, in which case you will need to think about those relative degrees of importance and weight each criterion accordingly.

- Thresholds are the lines between the degree neighborhoods on your standard. Let's say you have five degree neighborhoods (terrible, weak, okay, good, and super-good). As the song meets more and more of your individual criteria, its evaluation judgment will move away from the lower neighborhoods (out of terrible and even weak) and into the better neighborhood (perhaps all the way up to super-good). You will need to determine what it takes (how many criteria must be met and how well) in order for the evaluative judgment to cross the threshold from one neighborhood and into the next higher neighborhood.

Now that you have worked through the increasing challenges in this five-part structure, you can work through it again with other media messages. Use this structure to create additional examples. Start with relatively easier challenges (such as an advertising claim or fact in a news story to be evaluated for accuracy or trustworthiness) and move on up to more significant challenges (such as the entertainment value of a video series or the artistic value of a Hollywood movie director).

Grouping
Classifying Elements in Media Messages

The grouping skill is used to sort through an assortment of elements to determine how they can be arranged into meaningful sets such that the elements in each set share significant similarities while the elements across sets exhibit significant differences. Thus the grouping skill involves contrasting and comparing. *Contrasting* is looking for differences across elements; these differences are what you use to put the elements into different groups. *Comparing* is looking for commonalities across elements; these commonalities are what you use to argue that the elements you have put into the same group do in fact belong together. Those differences and similarities reveal classification rules.

Sometimes the classification rules are fully specified before the sorting begins; in this case, the grouping task is relatively easy because the challenge is to keep an adequate level of concentration in applying those *a priori* rules. The challenge becomes more difficult when the rules are not fully specified before the sorting begins; in this case, the person using the grouping skill will need to refine the rules during the sorting process so that all elements can be grouped in a nonarbitrary manner. The challenge of grouping is most difficult when the person doing the grouping does not start the task with any classification rules and must develop these rules while engaged in the grouping. While this is difficult, it is still possible and, in fact, is a common practice.

The skill of grouping allows us to reduce a relatively large number of elements down into a smaller set of meaningful groups, which helps us deal with the flow of information more efficiently. More importantly, each time we use the skill of grouping, we have an opportunity to learn something about *how* we organize knowledge. That is, as we make our decisions about which of the characteristics among elements are the most meaningful, we gain insights about which characteristics we regard as most important. This tells us what we regard as the essential differences and similarities across the elements we are examining. When we use this skill well, we are building significant understanding about the nature of the set of elements.

I. The Grouping Algorithm

The skill of grouping is essentially a process of five steps (Table 5.1). If you are given a clear and complete set of classification rules, then you can skip the first three steps listed below because someone else has already done this

TABLE 5.1	The Skill of Grouping

Purpose: To determine which elements are alike in some way and to determine which elements are different in some way

Pre-Task: Conduct an analysis to identify message elements.

Algorithm:

1. List all possible classification schemes that could guide the grouping of message elements.

2. Determine your purpose for the compare/contrast.

3. Select the most appropriate classification scheme(s) to fulfill your purpose.

4. Use the classification scheme to place each message element in its proper category. At this point, you have conducted a one-level analysis.

5. Examine configurations in the groupings.

work for you. However, even when you are given classification rules before you begin, there are times when you might find that the rules you were given are not complete enough or clear enough to finish the task with confidence. In this case, you may need to cycle back through some of the first three steps. Now, let's look at each of these five steps.

Step 1: List All Possible Classification Schemes

Typically, the best place to begin this process of grouping is to think about the elements you want to group and list all the possible ways those elements could be arranged into groups. Of course, you may already have an idea about how you want to group the elements, so this brainstorming step of listing all the possible classification schemes really serves to open your mind to alternatives. You might find that one of these alternatives turns out to be a better choice than your initial scheme. Or if you end up realizing that your initial scheme was better than the alternatives, then you have confidence that you are beginning on the right track. Like with the skills of analysis and evaluation, it is better to begin with an examination of your options before committing to one purpose. When you consider your range of options early in the process of using a skill, you typically end up applying the skill in a manner that better serves your needs than if you had locked yourself into an initially "dreamed up" option.

For example, look at Figure 5.1. The elements in this figure can be grouped in several different ways. One way is by shading; we would end up with three groups of black, gray, and white. Or we could group by shape and again end up with three groups of triangle, circle, and square. Or we could group by size and end up with one group of larger elements and a second group of smaller elements. Or we could put the two red circles together and put everything else into a miscellaneous pile. This illustrates that there are

FIGURE 5.1   Classifying Objects

Large Black Triangle	Large Gray Circle	Large White Square
Small Black Circle	Small Gray Square	Small White Triangle
Large Gray Square	Small White Triangle	Small Black Circle

many ways that a collection of elements can be arranged into groups. The way you do the grouping depends on which characteristics of the elements you regard as most important for your purpose.

As another example, let's consider the classification schemes that can be used to compare and contrast media messages. A characteristic that has often been used in the past to group media messages has been by medium. Using this characteristic of medium, we would have a group for books, newspapers, magazines, recordings, films, radio, broadcast television, and cable television. If we were back in the 1950s to 1970s, this set of groups would work well to include all media messages and it would be very easy to put every media message into one and only one group accurately. However, the media environment has changed so much over the past 5 decades that the characteristic of medium is almost useless. For example, if this were 1970, then it would be easy to put the media message of NBC News into the broadcast television category; but now NBC News could be put into several categories: broadcast television, cable television, and Internet. The changes in the media environment have rendered the idea of medium as far less useful than other characteristics of messages. Likewise, genre used to be a good classification scheme for grouping media messages. Decades ago, it was relatively easy to group media messages by entertainment, news/information, and advertising. But over time, the hard edges of these categories have eroded as previously distinct content types blended together. For example, many news reports look like entertainment messages with the use of simulations, music, and appeals to the emotions. Many ads look like news reports to mislead audiences into believing that the persuasive claims are objective reporting.

A classification scheme that is better than medium or genre is **vehicle**. Media vehicles are the mechanisms that deliver the media messages. For example, on the Internet we get very different kinds of messages from the vehicles of Google, Amazon, Facebook, ESPN, *World of Warcraft*, *Huffington Post*, and so on. Within any medium, there is a variety of vehicles. Making comparisons across vehicles can reveal the differences and similarities of editorial perspectives, business constraints, and their perspective on audiences. But using vehicle as a classification scheme also has its limitations. To see for yourself that not all magazines are alike, compare a nonfiction story in *Time*, *Cosmopolitan*, and *Soldier of Fortune*.

Other possible classification schemes for media messages are time, region, and author/producer. There are many, many possibilities for classification schemes. Making a choice of classification becomes easier to the extent that you have a clear purpose.

Step 2: Determine Your Purpose for the Compare/Contrast

Once you understand the options for your grouping, the second step is to commit to a purpose to guide your comparing and contrasting. Again like with the task of analysis and evaluation, grouping is a tool that needs to be guided by a plan or goal. You must ask yourself why you are doing the grouping. Typically the grouping task is guided by the dimensions you used to analyze the information.

Step 3: Select the Most Appropriate Classification Scheme(s)

The third step is to select the most appropriate **classification scheme**(s) to fulfill your purpose. There are almost always many classification schemes to consider, but not all of them are equally useful. In selecting a classification scheme, you must consider the purpose for the grouping.

Let's consider an example. Imagine that I show you three objects: a red ball, a pear, and a knife. Then I ask you which of the three objects is like an apple. You could pick the red ball, saying that both share the same shape and color. Or you could pick the pear, reasoning that both are examples of fruit. Or you could pick the knife, thinking that you use a knife to pare the apple before eating it. Which of these three is correct? They all are, because there is a reason to group each one with the apple. But which grouping is the most meaningful and shows you understand the nature of the comparison? In order to answer this question, you need more context. Let's say I asked this question in a nutrition class; the answer would likely be the pear because they are both fruit and therefore the apple's nutrients most closely match that of the pear. But if I asked this question in a drawing class, the answer would be the red ball, because the apple's shape and color most closely match that of the ball. Context and purpose are important to the use of the skill of grouping. When a person is aware of the purpose of the grouping and employs a good context, the use of the grouping skill can generate understanding of the nature of the elements.

Step 4: Categorize the Elements

In this step, begin by examining a message for elements that would allow you to place it in one of the categories of your classification scheme. You have likely identified these elements in an analysis. Translate this into a decision rule that guides you in the categorization. The simplest decision rule is this: When a message has an X characteristic, it gets put into the X group; if the message has a Y characteristic, it gets put into the Y group. Your decision rule should be clear, but that is not enough; the set of decision rules needs to be complete. In the above example, the rule set is not complete because it does not indicate what needs to be done when an element exhibits both X and Y. What should we do if an element does not exhibit either characteristic?

Once you categorize the first message, continue this categorization process until all messages are in a group. Those messages that are in the same group have been compared; that is, they all share the same key characteristic. The messages that differ by grouping have been contrasted; that is, they differ on the key characteristic. (See the noncategorical scheme heuristic.)

Step 5: Examine Configurations in the Groupings

The final step in applying the grouping skill is to check your groupings to see if they make sense. Sometimes we get so wrapped up in the details of placing individual messages into groups that we lose sight of the big picture. So once your groupings are done, stand back and see if there are any messages in a group that do not look like they belong there. For example, if you are grouping television shows on the element of degree of violence in the shows, you will have one category labeled "highly violent" that includes crime programs and action/adventure shows. But this same category is also likely to include cartoons, *The Jerry Springer Show*, and local news programs. You must ask yourself if this grouping makes sense. If the answer is yes, then you need to be clear with your reasoning so that you can defend your groupings to critics. If the answer is no—the elements in that one group do not all belong together—then you need to re-examine your decision rule. Were you sloppy in using that decision rule to place messages into groups? Or was the decision rule itself faulty?

II. Heuristics

The skill of grouping appears very simple. After all, people seem to be able to use this skill at a very early age. Even toddlers group people (strangers and familiar people), things (those that move and those that do not), and places (home and not home). As people grow older, they are constantly faced with grouping tasks. Many of these tasks are fairly challenging, although they may not appear so until we really examine them.

We use many heuristics with the skill of grouping. In fact, without heuristics, we would not be able to complete many grouping tasks at all. The importance of heuristics became apparent when scientists working on artificial intelligence (AI) began programming computers to emulate the human mind and found the task of grouping to be an enormously challenging one. Computers are programmed with algorithms and slavishly follow those programmed rules. However, when a computer does not have enough rules to complete a task, it gets stuck and cannot finish the task. The computer cannot figure a way out of a dead-end. It cannot think laterally or acquire information through intuition or insight. Humans can do these things and thus can complete very challenging grouping tasks. But in order to do this, we need heuristics. This section presents five heuristics that can help with the most common challenges of using the grouping skill: (1) the **emerging classification scheme heuristic,** (2) the **primitive classification heuristic,** (3) the **noncategorical scheme heuristic,** (4) the **multiple characteristics heuristic,** and (5) the **how many groups? heuristic.**

Heuristic 1: Emerging Classification Scheme

There may be times when you can think of no classification schemes before conducting this task. Therefore, you have no guidance. But a classification scheme is essential, and you cannot complete this task without one. So you must develop the scheme while you are doing the grouping. This is the most challenging form of the classification task.

To illustrate this, let's say you attend the first meeting of 10 courses at your university and you want to group the professors in those courses in terms of the messages they present about themselves. There is no *a priori* category scheme that you could look up that would tell you the different categories of messages professors use during the first meeting of their classes. So you take notes on what the 10 professors each say about themselves. You read your notes and look for differences and similarities in their messages. Let's say you notice that a few of the professors say nothing about themselves; this becomes one category. Of those who do reveal things about themselves, you notice that some limit their remarks to their role as a professor; they talk about what they personally hope to achieve in the course and tell stories about how they designed the course and what student behavior makes them happy. The other professors seem to get more personal and tell you stories about their family and their interests outside of teaching. These three categories are derived inductively by first examining the messages and looking for patterns—in this case, similarities and differences in professors' use of personal information across those messages. You end up with a *post hoc* three-category scheme. The challenge here is building the scheme while you are doing the comparing and contrasting. The category scheme is a product of the grouping process itself.

Heuristic 2: Primitive Classification

When we are very young, we typically learn classification by observing objects and having someone (such as parents) tell us what the categories of things are. They point to things and say the name of a category. For example, they point to something and say "dog," then point to something else and say "chair," and point to something else and say "cat." As we associate these names of categories with objects, we intuitively learn the characteristics that make things different or the same. This is a primitive scheme because it often resists the articulation of the kind of rules that could be written down and transferred through instruction. Instead it is more intuitive than systematic. However, this procedure typically works well in everyday life. For example, few people have a problem classifying objects as being either a chair or not a chair. Yet we never learned a formal definition for chair, nor did we learn any formal process that would guide the classification. This claim may sound wrong, but try writing down your definition for chair. Then use what you have on the paper to classify things like stools, ottomans, rocking chairs, high chairs, armchairs, wing-back chairs, folding chairs, three-legged chairs, benches, chaise lounges, couches, love seats, and recliners. You will notice that while you fully understand the concept of chair and can make endless decisions without error in classifying objects as a chair or not, it is still impossible to articulate a good definition. Classifying objects as being a chair or not is a partially specified problem. We have no decision-making flow chart that can guide us in such a classification task.

When we see an object, we use the characteristics of things we have already learned to make a guess at what the object is—that is, to which category of things it belongs. Often, when we are new to an area, we will choose a wrong or peripheral characteristic to make the classification and the classification will be wrong. If a parent (or someone experienced in classification) is around to correct us, we can learn by trial and error. Over time we come to understand the essential characteristics of things in different categories.

The key to grouping is to know what the essential criteria are in the classification scheme. Let's say I tell you I am looking at an animal that is four legged and black; it has two eyes and a pointed nose and is as tall as my knee, wagging its tail and wearing a collar with a leash hanging off it. You would likely classify this as a dog. But how did you make such a classification? You took into consideration all the details, and they fit the pattern that you have learned about dog; that is, there is nothing in the set of details that does not fit the schema elements for dog. You also need structure in the elements to make the classification efficiently and accurately. The first detail—*animal*—keyed you to a path that this is a living thing but not a plant. *Four legged* allowed you to rule out all bipeds. *Black* is a peripheral characteristic not critical in this classification task. *Two eyes* could be relevant but at this point in the reasoning process, it adds no information that could make a finer discrimination. *Pointed nose* rules out cats, as does the height (*tall as my knee*). Finally, the *wagging tail* and *collar with a leash* indicate that the animal is domesticated. All of these bits of information about the object have delivered you to a point where you identify with confidence that the object belongs in the dog group, although you did not access a simple rule to make that classification.

Heuristic 3: Noncategorical Scheme

There are times when the characteristic upon which you build your classification scheme is not categorical; that is, an element has some of the characteristics in order for it to be put into a particular group but is also missing some of the other characteristics that the classification scheme requires. In this case, you have three options. One option is to group this element with the other elements that have all the characteristics and tell yourself that this is close enough; the classification is not important enough for you to worry about "minor" exceptions. A second option is to group it with the other elements that have none of the characteristics and label that category as "miscellaneous." And the third option is to create another category for those elements that have some but not all of the characteristics. If you select the third option, then you have the problem of deciding if all elements that have some of the characteristic belong in the same group; some of those elements may have a lot—but not all—of the characteristics, while other elements may have a little of the characteristic. Should you create several new categories? If so, how many categories? The challenge here is to transform what is a continuum of degrees of the characteristic into a set of categories.

To illustrate what this type of challenge entails, let's say you want to group front-page newspaper stories on the characteristic of length. There is no natural category system for short length, medium length, and long length. There is a natural continuum of column inches or words. You could create a category system by arbitrarily cutting up the continuum; for example, short articles are 1 to 5 column inches, medium stories are more than 5 but less than 12 column inches, and long stories are 12 column inches or longer. Thus you have met the challenge of lacking a natural category system for you classification scheme by creating your own set of categories.

However, the category scheme created in the previous paragraph might bother you because it is arbitrary; that is, why should a story that is 6 column inches be considered short, while a story of 7 column inches is considered medium? There is no way to eliminate the arbitrary nature of translating a natural continuum of values into categories. But there is a way to make it seem less arbitrary by constructing the categories in such a way that there are few elements at the cut-points that form the boundaries of the categories. Returning to our example with classifying the size of newspaper stories, you could measure the length of each story and plot it first before constructing your categories. Let's say you do this with news stories and plot each one on the continuum of column inches and find that there are clusters of stories at 5 to 7 inches, another cluster at 10 to 12 inches, and a third cluster at 20 to 24 inches. The results show three clusters (short, medium, and long) and this gives you the ability to conclude that there are three groups. But notice that if you had used the *a priori* clustering scheme, you would have divided the first cluster (5 to 7 inches) into short- and medium-length stories; thus, a minor difference in length resulted in a large difference in category. At the same time at the other end of the continuum, stories of 12 inches and 24 inches (a large difference in length) are both classified in the same category (long stories). If you must translate a continuous distribution of characteristics into a categorical classification scheme, which you frequently do, then it is better to look at how the elements cluster on the continuum before deciding on how many categories you will have and where the boundaries of the categories should be.

Heuristic 4: Multiple Characteristics

The simplest form of compare/contrast is to make decisions on only one key characteristic. When you do your grouping on one characteristic, your comparing and contrasting is likely to result in a fairly simple and defensible set of groups of elements.

But sometimes it makes more sense to consider more than one characteristic simultaneously, and the process of grouping becomes more complex as each additional characteristic is added to the task. With only one characteristic guiding the grouping, it is relatively easy to set up the classification scheme. When you involve two characteristics in the classification scheme, it becomes a bit more complicated but it is still relatively simple. You can draw a two-dimensional matrix and plot the elements in the two-dimensional space. Where elements cluster together, draw a circle around them and consider each circled area a grouping. Humans can also use this procedure to group on three characteristics simultaneously and envision the result, with elements occupying neighborhoods in the three-dimensional cube. But when we get beyond three dimensions, humans lose the capacity to envision the clustering, because it is very difficult to "see" things clustered in more than three-dimensional space. This leads to a risk that the resulting groupings, along say five dimensions, may result in some strange-looking sets of elements. For example, let's say you wanted to compare/contrast American universities. You could group according to whether the university was public or private, cost of tuition (high, medium, or low), and rejection rates (high, medium, or low). With these three categories it would still be possible to graphically envision the clusterings of elements.

But let's say that you wanted to group American universities on "best buys"—that is, where you get the most for your money. In order to do this, you would need to group on the characteristics of both cost and benefits simultaneously. If you grouped only on cost, you would construct a group of relatively inexpensive universities, but you would end up putting universities with many benefits in the same category as universities with few benefits. Also, if you grouped only on benefits, you could construct a group of universities that provide a relatively high number of benefits to students but you would end up putting super-expensive universities in the same category as those universities that are relatively inexpensive. In this example, any grouping based on only a single characteristic would not result in meaningful groups. Instead, you would need to take into consideration at least two characteristics (costs and benefits) simultaneously, and it is likely that the element of benefits would itself be composed of several subelements (faculty/student ratio, number of majors and courses offered, percentage of students going to graduate school or professional careers of their choice, etc.). The grouping procedure then must employ multiple characteristics simultaneously.

There are two major challenges of using a classification scheme of multiple characteristics. One of these major challenges is concerned with determining which characteristics should be included in the classification scheme. In the above example, it is obvious that there are many ways of defining a benefit of college. Do we include only academic benefits, such as the resources of classes, professors, library, computer, and so on? Do we include nonacademic benefits, such as quality of the dorms, number and kind of social clubs, sports activities, weather, and so forth? Do we limit ourselves to the college-attending years or do we include outcomes of the education, such as ability to get a job and level of earning 5 years after graduation? Also, the cost characteristic itself suggests subelements of tuition, room and board (reflects cost of living in the campus area), and miscellaneous charges (fees not included in tuition such as the technology fee, student activity fee, parking, books and other instructional materials, etc.)

The second challenge of using a classification scheme with multiple characteristics is making a summary judgment when using many characteristics simultaneously. Should all characteristics be weighted equally in making the summary judgment? In our university example, maybe the cost factors should be weighted about the same as the benefit factors, but within the cost factors, perhaps tuition should be weighted most heavily. Maybe the presence of one characteristic cancels out the effect of another characteristic? Again with our example, perhaps a university has many academic and nonacademic benefits on campus, but none of its graduates can get jobs or get accepted to graduate schools. In this case, the lack of student postgraduate success might cancel out all of the benefits on campus.

Many of the important decisions we must make in life require us to use our grouping skill and to consider multiple characteristics in the things we are grouping. This is not an easy task. If we have high anxiety and want to make our groupings as quickly as possible so we can arrive at a decision and reduce our anxiety, then we are likely to take shortcuts by not thinking through all the decisions we should make systematically. We may achieve efficiency but it will come at the expense of effectiveness.

Heuristic 5: How Many Groups?

How many groups should we end up with? It is impossible to provide a general answer to this question. It depends on the nature of the elements you are trying to group. If those elements only have one characteristic and that characteristic has only two values, then you really only have two possibilities for grouping. For example, let's say you have a dozen batteries on a table. The typical reason you would want to group these objects is according to whether they have any power left or not. If they work, you put them in one pile and save them. If they do not work, you put them in another pile and throw them away.

Almost all elements have several different characteristics that you could use to group them. Let's return to the battery example. Besides whether they work or not, the batteries also have a size (AAAA, AAA, AA, A, B, C, D, etc.), they have a brand (Eveready, Duracell, etc.), and they have a voltage rating (1.5 volts, 9 volts, etc.). Once you have selected a characteristic on which to group, the values available on that characteristic will limit the number of groups you could have.

While the number of values on a particular characteristic will usually determine the number of groups you work with, there are some elements that have no obvious number of values. In this situation, the number of groups is likely to be determined by you either given your goal or your cognitive traits, especially when it comes to your trait of conceptual differentiation. Some people tend to group all things together unless they are radically different from one another. Other people like to create lots of neat little groupings. It is a personality feature. Think of your sock drawer. Do you have all your socks thrown in together? Or do you have them lined up in lots of groups according to color, pattern, style, or purpose (dress, casual, athletic, etc.)?

III. Avoiding Traps

The two traps discussed in this section illuminate problems that are opposite to each other. Sometimes everything looks the same to you and you cannot see more than one group, and this group includes every message. Other times, you cannot see much similarity across any messages and think that each message must be its own group. Both of these are traps if they prevent you from reaching your goal for grouping. No matter how alike all messages at first seem, there are differences across them. On the other hand, no matter how unique each message seems, there are similarities.

To illustrate the grouping problem, let's consider what marketers do in grouping the population of this country of 330 million people. At the individual level, each of us is unique; no two of us dress, act, and think identically to anyone else—even twins! In addition to our differences, we share some commonalities. If we were to group people by age, it would make sense to put all people age 15 to 18, for example, in one group and find lots of commonalities in the way they dress, the music they listen to, and the way they spend their time. Of course, everyone in this age group is not identical on these characteristics, but the commonalities are far more consistent than they would be if we tried to put people age 50 to 55 into this same group.

Given any set of elements, it is possible to argue that they are all alike in some way and it is also possible to argue that they are all different in some way. This is possible as an academic exercise, but when faced with a grouping challenge, the key is to be aware of your purpose for the grouping, and this will almost always require you to move away from the extremes and find a middle number of groups.

Trap 1: Everything Is the Same

Oftentimes you will not be able to find ways that messages are different from one another, because everything looks the same to you. In this case, you need to list all the characteristics that make them look the same to you. As you make this list, other characteristics may occur to you and these may be characteristics that differentiate among the messages. Let's say this does not happen spontaneously. What do you do? One thing you can do is to list the opposites of the characteristics on your list. Now you have two lists. Are there any messages that maybe have characteristics on your opposite list? Perhaps you could gather more messages and when you do, you find there are messages that do.

If the above techniques do not work for you, then try what I call the "elephant technique." Think about an elephant and how it is different from all the elements you are trying to subdivide into groups. For example, let's say you are trying to divide the music of Britney Spears into groups, and all of her songs sound the same to you; that is, you just can't see any differences that would allow you to put her songs into separate groups. Think of an elephant. How is an elephant different than her songs? One way is that an elephant is alive and music is not a living thing. Literally this is true, but how could this be used to perceive differences in her music? Perhaps some of her songs are livelier than others. Think of an elephant moving around; it is slow and ponderous. Perhaps some of Britney Spears's music is slow paced and other songs are faster paced. The ground vibrates when an elephant walks. Perhaps some songs have a stronger bass beat than others. The value of the elephant technique is that it gets you far away from the set of things you are trying to subdivide and gives you a very different perspective on those elements by forcing you to make ridiculous comparisons. Yet those ridiculous comparisons will get you thinking in a lateral way and perhaps get you around the barrier that has trapped your thinking.

There is one more note about the elephant technique: you don't have to think about an elephant to use the technique. The "elephant" can be anything radically different from the set of elements you are trying to subdivide. It can be your grandmother's false teeth, the sound a bee makes, the smell of a month-old piece of pizza, the idea of long division, or a French kiss. Be creative with your elephant!

Trap 2: Everything Is Different

Some people are overanalytical. Recall from Chapter 2 on knowledge styles that people vary in terms of their conceptual differentiation. Some people tend to group all things together unless those things are radically different from one another. Other people like to create lots of neat little groupings. The way we go about grouping reveals interesting characteristics about our personalities. Again, think of your sock drawer. If you have a high need to group and organize, you keep analyzing the characteristics of things until you find enough idiosyncratic characteristics to make them all seem unique. Perhaps this is a good thing if you want to have the same number of categories as messages, and each category contains one and only one message. However, this is rare.

The payoff of using the grouping skill well is to end up with a smaller number of groups than messages. This allows you to organize a large number of things (messages) into a small number of categories. This provides efficiency.

To avoid this trap of seeing every element as different from one another, focus more on similarities than differences. Randomly choose two elements from all the elements you must group. Force yourself to see something the two elements have in common. Then look to see how many other elements have that same thing in common. If you find that a good percentage of elements have that thing in common, then that characteristic could be used as a classification rule. What is a "good percentage"? I would say somewhere between 10% and 50%. If you find more than half the elements share the characteristic, then the characteristic is not a fine enough discriminator. If less than 10% share the characteristic, then perhaps it is too trivial of a commonality to use as a grouping rule.

IV. Chapter Review

- Grouping is a skill with which we have had much practice. However, we have learned many of the classification schemes and rules for categorization through trial and error, which is very time-consuming. A more efficient way to be successful with a grouping task is to follow the five-step algorithm presented in this chapter. Also, be warned that many grouping tasks are partially specified, so it is important that you take advantage of the heuristics. Finally, avoid the typical traps that prevent us from being successful with grouping.

- Formal education is likely to teach classification by presenting a set of rules rather than using the example method. Our educational system has limited resources and therefore cannot hire teachers to follow students around and give them copious personal feedback on the trial-and-error process. Therefore, teachers need to present rules. Some topics, such as math and science, are easy to teach with rules, while others are much harder to teach with rules, such as appreciation of the arts or understanding the vast variety of human behavior.

Exercise 5.1   Practice Using the Grouping Algorithm

This is a sequence of four challenges designed to increase your understanding of using your skill of grouping. This sequence starts with the easiest challenges by providing you with the maximum degree of guidance. As you progress through this sequence, you will find the exercises increasingly challenging because you will have to do more of the thinking for yourself.

Challenge I

Think about your favorite video series and use the skill of grouping to classify the characters in that series.

1. Use the classification scheme that has three groupings:

   Major Characters — appear on every episode; plot focuses on their actions

   Supporting Characters — appear on most episodes; they support or antagonize the major characters

   Peripheral Characters — appear on one or a small number of episodes as background; these are characters such as waiters in restaurants, taxi drivers, clerks, and so on.

2. Put each character into one and only one group.

Challenge II

Think about your favorite video series and use the skill of grouping to classify the characters in that series.

1. Use a classification scheme of gender with two categories of female and male.

2. Your purpose for the grouping is to determine the gender balance in your favorite video series. You want to find out if the number of female characters in your favorite video series matches the number of characters who are male—as is the balance in real life.

3. Classify each element. This grouping procedure should be fairly easy unless you also have to classify nonhumans such as animals or inanimate objects.

4. Examine configurations in the groupings. Are you satisfied with all your groupings? If not, then cycle back through the previous steps.

(Continued)

(Continued)

Challenge III

Think about your favorite video series and use the skill of grouping to classify the characters in that series.

1. Use a classification scheme of age.

2. Your purpose for the grouping is to determine the age distribution in your favorite video series. You want to find out if the characteristic of age has a wide or narrow range and if there is a cluster where most characters are the same age.

3. Decide how you will classify age. This is your decision.

   • Will you try to estimate each character's age? This will be difficult to do with precision.

   • Or will you set up age categories? If so, what will those age categories be?

4. Classify each character by age.

5. Examine configurations in the groupings. Now that you have grouped all the characters in your favorite video series on age, are there any decisions you made that you need to "second guess" or are you confident with all your decisions? If you are less than confident, go back through the first four steps again and see if you can change your purpose or classification rules to end up with groupings with which you have more.

Challenge IV

Think about your favorite video series and use the skill of grouping to classify the characters in that series.

1. List all possible classification schemes beyond the ones suggested in the exercises above.

2. Determine your purpose for the compare/contrast. This is your decision.

3. Select the most appropriate classification scheme(s). This is your decision.

4. Classify each element.

5. Examine configurations in the groupings. Now that you have grouped all the characters in your favorite video series, are there any decisions you made that you need to "second guess" or are you confident with all your decisions? If you are less than confident, go back through the first four steps again and see if you can change your purpose or classification rules to end up with groupings with which you have more confidence.

Exercise 5.2 Observe How Other People Group Things

1. Go to your professor's office and look at how the books are arranged. Are there sections for different kinds of books or are the books simply in one group arranged alphabetically?

2. Look at your roommate's side of the room. There is likely to be a group of things on a desk, another group on a dresser, and another group on a night table. Can you see what all the objects in one group have in common with one another? Can you see why there are differences across groups (why an object obviously belongs in one particular group and not the others)?

3. Go to a grocery store and walk down the soft drink aisle. How are the products grouped? Is it by brand? Is it by size? Is it by type (all the diet drinks together, all colas together, etc.)? Why do you think they are grouped the way they are?

   Walk down the aisle with cereals. How are cereals grouped as they are displayed on the shelves? Are cereals grouped by the same classification rules as are soft drinks?

   Look at how other products are grouped on grocery store shelves. Can you see any general classification rules that apply to the grouping of all products?

4. Think about how knowledge is organized at your college.

   Think of the physical sciences. How many are there? What are the differences between each of those groups? For example, what makes biology different from chemistry?

   Now think about the humanities. How many groups are there within the humanities? What are the differences between those groups?

   Now think of the arts. How many groups are there within the arts? What are the differences between those groups?

   Now think about the bigger picture. You have broken the physical sciences down into groups. You have done the same to the humanities and the arts. If physical sciences, humanities, and the arts are three big macro groups of knowledge on campus, what are the other macro groups?

Exercise 5.3 Observe How You Typically Group Things

1. List about a dozen names of friends on a piece of paper.

   Arrange those friends in groups. One arrangement is to group by gender; put all males in one group labeled "males" and all females in another group labeled "females." This arrangement has two groups. How many different arrangements can you make?

2. On a piece of paper, list all the things you like about college.

   Arrange those things in groups. How many different arrangements can you make?

3. Think about the student body at your college. Most colleges are mixes of different types of students. One type found at most campuses is the "jock" or athlete.

   How many distinct groups of students can you make from the student body at your school?

   For each group, what are the things all students in that group share? List the adjectives that would apply to all members of that group.

   In which student group are you? Do you share most of the characteristics as the other members of that group? If so, you are a prototypical member. If you only share a few characteristics with the other members of your group, perhaps you should create a new group with you as its prototypical member. How many members (besides you) are there in this new group?

4. Think about your groupings of students (from question 3 in this exercise) and your groupings of knowledge (from question 4 in Exercise 5.2).

   Do you see any match between a particular group of student and a particular group of knowledge? If so, what are the characteristics in that student group that match up so well with the characteristics of the knowledge group?

5. Think about how you spend your time during a typical day. How many groups would you need to categorize your time?

   For each group, list the activities that count. For example, if "going to class" is one of your groups, does the time spent walking to class count? Does talking to your professor after class count? Where do you draw the line about what gets put into this group?

   List your groups of time. For each group, estimate the amount of time you spend in that time group on a typical day.

   Test your groups. Tomorrow as you go through your day, carry a sheet of paper with you so you can write down each thing you do and how much time you spend with it. At the end of the day, arrange those activities and times into your time groups. As you do this, you may want to modify your rules for what goes into a group; you may even want to rename groups or even reconfigure the groups themselves.

Inducing

Looking For Patterns Within and Across Media Messages

We use the skill of induction when we draw general conclusions about elements after making a small set of observations about those elements. For example, let's say you watch a video in which a young child throws a temper tantrum. Then later you are in a store and see a young child whining because his father won't buy him some candy. You find yourself thinking "All children are so spoiled these days!" After you have experienced only two instances of children behaving badly, you have inferred a pattern (both children were spoiled) and generalized that pattern to all children. In essence, *induction* is the skill of inferring a pattern among a few observations and then generalizing that pattern.

The skill of induction is important for media literacy because we are continually drawing conclusions about all kinds of things we experience in media messages. We watch news coverage of several politicians lying to the public and draw a conclusion that all politicians are dishonest. We watch a few episodes of a new video series, observe the way the characters behave, then draw conclusions about how they will behave in future episodes. The conclusions we construct from our small number of observations are speculations about a pattern that explain what we have perceived in those few observations. When we generalize that speculated pattern, we are in essence creating a belief that the pattern holds across many situations that we have not observed. These beliefs we construct through induction then become our standards when we evaluate all kinds of experiences in the media as well as all kinds of things in real life. If those beliefs were constructed too hastily from a few idiosyncratic experiences, then the faulty nature of those beliefs will have a negative cascading effect as we use those faulty beliefs to guide how we make decisions and how we live our lives.

All of us want a good amount of useful knowledge about how the world works, but we cannot possibly experience everything the world has to offer. Our experience is always limited. No matter how many people we meet, we will never be able to meet everyone; yet we want to feel that we understand human behavior. The skill of induction is a tool we use to make sense of our experiences and to leverage what we learn from those experiences into general principles about how the world works.

Induction is the skill we employ when we use the *scientific method*. Remember learning this in high school? With the scientific method, we first pose a question, then make observations to find an answer to our question. As we make our observations, we look for patterns that could provide an answer to our question. When we see a pattern, we continue to make observations to see if this initial claim for a pattern holds up. As additional observations continue to support our initial claim, our confidence grows that this pattern will continue to hold up, so we generalize this claim; that is, we use this claim to explain all kinds of situations, events, and people, beyond those we have observed.

Psychologists often refer to people as **naïve scientists** because of the way we approach problem solving in our everyday lives. In this term, the word *scientists* refers to our use of the scientific method, and the word *naïve* refers to our lack of knowledge about the full power of induction as well as its limitations. Of course, when we confront most of our everyday challenges, we do not need to know the full power of induction or be wary of its limitations. In everyday life, we are motivated by efficiency; therefore, we want to perceive patterns as quickly as possible and then move on to other things. The consequences of being wrong are slight, so we are motivated more by efficiency than by accuracy.

In other situations, however, when being right is more important than speed alone, we become motivated more by accuracy than by efficiency. When we are guided by the goal of accuracy, we need to know more about the process of induction and how to get the most out of it. We need to be more systematic in how we use this skill and avoid traps that will lead us to inaccurate conclusions. You already know how to use the skill of induction to achieve efficiency. The information in this chapter will help you develop your skill of induction in order to achieve the goal of accuracy.

I. The Induction Algorithm

Induction is a process of formulating a question, determining the element, making observations, inferring a pattern, generalizing the pattern, then continuing to test your claim of a pattern (Table 6.1). Because we live in an information-saturated society, we are continually making observations; we cannot avoid doing so. Therefore, the inductive process starts not when we make observations. Instead, the inductive process really starts when something grabs our attention in a way that stimulates us to begin asking questions about what is really going on, and we seek an explanation.

Step 1: Formulate a Question

The process of induction begins while you are making observations and some kind of question occurs to you about those observations. For example, you come across a political blog and begin reading the comments that are posted there by a person calling himself Horatio. You notice that Horatio

TABLE 6.1	The Skill of Inducing

Purpose: To infer patterns across individual observations

Algorithm:

1. Formulate a question.

2. Determine the element to observe.

3. Make observations of several elements of a given type.

4. Infer a pattern. Look for commonalities across those elements to make a claim about a pattern.

5. Generalize a pattern. Claim the pattern holds throughout the full set of elements from which you made your few observations.

6. Continue to test your claim. The additional observations will either support your pattern, which will increase your confidence in the accuracy of your general claim, or not support your pattern, which falsifies the general claim. With falsification, we can either reject the entire general claim or alter it so that it is less general—that is, so the claim is no longer so broad that it includes the nonsupportive observations.

presents some very strong and controversial arguments and that he supports those arguments with facts and figures that do not seem accurate to you. A question arises in your mind: Can I trust Horatio's arguments?

Sometimes your question is more fully formed. For example, let's say you watch a local television newscast and notice that the first few stories presented dealt with crime and violence that made you feel fear. You also notice that as the newscast continued, the type of stories seemed to shift into things that made you feel comfortable and happy (human interest stories, diversions, sports, weather). It occurs to you that there might be a relationship between part of the newscast and type of story, where news shows try to grab your attention by scaring you then shift the tone of their stories to make you feel good. You wonder if all newscasts begin by hooking viewers with fear then proceed to make them feel happy with humorous or uplifting stories.

Step 2: Determine the Element to Observe

The next step is to figure out what you need to observe across media messages. All media messages are clusters of many different elements. Not all elements are equally important to observe. In the Horatio example, we need to focus on the facts Horatio presents in his blog because we want to look for a pattern of accuracy. Although the fonts, colors, and pictures in Horatio's blog pages are all elements in those media messages, they are not relevant to our purpose. In the newscast example, our focus needs to be not on the stories themselves but on the emotions that are likely triggered in audiences.

Step 3: Make Observations

Your question sets up a need to make some observations. With the Horatio example, you check the accuracy of the facts and figures that he cites to support his arguments and you find that they are the same as the facts and figures you find in reputable sources, so you draw a conclusion about Horatio that he does good research and that his arguments can be trusted. Over the next week, you continue to read Horatio's comments and continue to check a fact here and there, always finding his facts to be accurate. With the newscast example, the question guides you to watch more newscasts and pay particular attention to the *types* of stories and how they may change in tone throughout the duration of the newscast.

The first two steps of this process of induction can be treated as a cycle that is repeated. This is especially the case when it is difficult to formulate a clear question initially. Perhaps you are motivated to engage in an induction process not because you have a clear question but because you have a nagging feeling. It may take several cycles of steps 1 and 2 to progress from the nagging feeling to the articulation of a clear question.

Step 4: Infer a Pattern

When you have a clear question and are making observations, you need to look for commonalities across those observations. This requires a careful examination of the elements you are observing.

Returning to the Horatio example, let's say that you have checked reputable sources for the facts that Horatio cites in his arguments and each time you find that his facts appear to be accurate. So you draw a conclusion about Horatio that he does good research and that his arguments can be trusted. This conclusion leads you to continue reading Horatio's blog, to trust the accuracy of his facts, and therefore to accept his opinions as valid. The more observations you make that confirm your speculation about a pattern, the more confidence you have that your inferred pattern is a correct explanation.

In the newscast example, you need to do a breadth analysis to identify the list of stories that are presented. Then you need to ask yourself if the same pattern of stories occurs in each newscast. Are the fear stories always presented first and never at the end of a news program? Are the humorous and human interest stories never presented first? Once this pattern occurs to you, you look at the sequence of stories in other newscasts to see if your guess at a pattern holds up in the other newscasts.

Let's say we watch a second newscast and perceive the same relationship between feelings of fear at the beginning and feelings of happiness at the end. You then watch a third, then a fourth newscast. In each newscast you see the same pattern of elements (sequence of stories). At this point in the inductive process, you have inferred a pattern: the initial stories evoke fear but then the later stories evoke positive emotions like happiness.

The process of pattern inference requires trial and error. You make some observations and notice some things occurring over and over. List those things. This list of commonalities is your initial pattern. Then add a few more observations and see which commonalities from the list should be retained and which should be deleted. Repeat this process over and over until it stabilizes—that is, the same commonalities consistently appear across all your observations.

This pattern is an inference that you have made from your observations. This inference only claims that a pattern is consistent across the elements you have observed. Returning to our newscast example, let's say you observed four particular newscasts, so the pattern is inferred from only those four newscasts. At this point, you make no claim that a fifth or sixth newscast would exhibit this pattern.

Step 5: Generalize the Pattern

The next step in this inductive process is to **generalize** the pattern; you claim that the pattern you inferred from your limited number of observations is not limited to only those observations but that it is more general; that is, you claim that the pattern holds across all possible elements, even those you have not observed. We elevate our initial claim (that there is a pattern across the observations we made) to a **general claim** (that the pattern exists across a broader set of elements that we have not observed).

Returning to the newscast example, we inferred a pattern across the four newscasts. However, we are more interested in *all* newscasts than we are interested in only four. If we generalize our pattern to all newscasts, we have a more interesting claim: All newscasts begin with stories of crime and violence to evoke fear in the audience and then shift to stories that will make the audience feel happy. This general claim gives us the sense that we know something about all newscasts without having to observe them all. Thus, we have created a general claim about all newscasts even though we only expended the effort to observe four.

With the Horatio example, what does generalizing mean? Let's say that you checked the accuracy of a dozen facts in a week's worth of his blog posting and you confirmed the accuracy of all those dozen facts. But let's also say that he reported 20 facts during that time, eight of which you did not check. A conservative generalization would be "Horatio can be trusted because he reported only accurate facts this week." This is relatively conservative because you are generalizing from 12 observations to a pattern across 20 elements (facts, in this case). A less conservative generalization is "I can trust all of Horatio's postings throughout the coming week." This is less conservative because you are using the 12 facts you checked in last week's posting to make a general claim that all the facts he will present in the coming week will also be accurate. An even less conservative generalization would be "I can always trust Horatio to present only accurate facts." And an even less conservative generalization would be "I can always trust anyone named Horatio at any time, in any situation." This is quite a generalization!

When we generalize, what we are doing, in essence, is removing the limitations of time, space, situation, and/or people. In our example, we removed the limitation of time by moving beyond four newscasts (accounting for about 2 hours of airtime) to all newscasts. Our general statement is not limited to four newscasts, 1 week of newscasts, newscasts only in the evening, newscasts only during sweeps months, newscasts only during one season of the year, or newscasts only this year. This statement is also very general as far as space; that is, it is not limited to newscasts in only one television market. Our generalization implies that the pattern holds in all 215 local markets in the United States; it also does not limit itself to only U.S. broadcast markets. And this statement is also very general as far as people; that is, it is not limited to only stories presented by people of one gender, age grouping, or ethnic background.

Step 6: Continue to Test Your Claim

Because your general claim was inferred from a small number of observations relative to the large number of observations that are theoretically possible, you need to continue making observations to see if the claim continues to hold. To do this efficiently, consider the dimensions you used to make your statement general—stretching on time, space, situation, and people. Select your messages strategically in those areas so as to maximize the return on your effort.

We could continue testing our general statement on the dimensions of time and space. The more testing we do, the more precisely we can craft our generalization and the more confidence we can have in the accuracy of that generalization. This testing step is what separates a good process of generalization from a poor one.

In everyday life, we frequently skip this step. When we are in a hurry or when the cost of making a wrong general claim is low, we do not continue to observe examples to see if our generalization holds. As a result, many of our general claims are wrong but we do not notice this. If our goal with induction is accuracy, then it is important to continue testing our generalizations so we can weed out the claims that initially generated support but later were found to have many exceptions. Even if we are very insightful in seeing patterns across as few as two messages, there is no guarantee that the pattern—no matter how brilliantly inferred—will show up in the third or 503rd observation. Therefore, the more observations we have to back up our inferred pattern, the more confidence we can have that our general claim accurately captures the pattern of all the elements in the set. How many observations are required? There is no way to answer this question in the abstract. For some guidelines on this point, see the falsification heuristic below.

II. Heuristics

More than any of the other seven skills, the tool of induction is least likely to be used with fully specified problems. The primary reason for this is that with few exceptions, the number of messages you would need to examine to support your claim completely would almost always be infinite. Generalizations can never be proven completely, because the number of observations that would have to be made in order to be complete is far too great. You may be asking "But if we can never make all the observations necessary, how can we ever know if the claim for a pattern we generalize is accurate?" The answer to this question is that we need some heuristics to help us increase our confidence in the claims we make. This section presents two heuristics to help you become comfortable with this problem that the algorithm by itself cannot resolve: (1) the **falsification heuristic** and (2) the **tentativeness heuristic**.

Heuristic 1: Falsification

You will never have absolute certainty that your general claim is accurate unless the number of elements in a given **population** is small enough that you can observe every one of those elements to make sure they all conform to your general claim. Almost all populations of elements are very large, so it is not possible to observe them all. Also some populations include elements that can never be observed. For example, if your generalization is not limited by time, then elements from the past are included in the set, and there is usually no way to make observations of those elements if they no longer exist. So your observations constitute a **sample** of elements from the full set of elements that compose the population of interest.

Why continue to test the accuracy of a general claim if it is not possible to fully confirm it? Even though you can never completely confirm the *accuracy* of a generalization, you can confirm the *inaccuracies*. As you continue to make observations of new elements, it is possible to find an exception to your pattern in the general claim. If you do find an exception, then the general claim is found to be faulty; that is, it is falsified. All it takes is one exception to falsify a general claim. Therefore, falsification is easier to demonstrate than is support, because full support would require that your sample of observations be as large as the population itself.

The power in falsification rests not so much in the negating of a pattern. That would be a pessimistic use, because it would invalidate all the work we did in making all the observations that supported the pattern in the general claim. Instead, the power in falsification lies in its ability to identify the boundaries of the pattern. Returning to our example about television newscasts, let's say that you viewed 99 newscasts and found every one of them to fit the pattern; then you view one that does not fit that pattern. Does this mean you have falsified the entire pattern and you must throw out all your work and start over? No, of course not. Instead, we have reached the boundary of the pattern. We need to examine the characteristics of the one newscast that does not fit the pattern and try to determine in what ways it is different from the other 99 newscasts. Perhaps, the 99 newscasts were all from United States television stations and the one that did not fit the pattern was from a Canadian television station. In this case, we have found the limit to the pattern and must revise our general claim, but before we do, it would be good to examine newscasts on other Canadian stations and also perhaps stations in Mexico and other countries. Depending on what we find, we may end up revising the generalizing of our pattern from "all television stations" to the more limited "United States television stations."

It is a good technique to use the power of falsification to test for the boundaries for generalizing your pattern. Think about what the pattern's limits might be in terms of time, place, situation, and people. Make observations of elements that test these limits. By doing this, you will be using your time well. When you find examples that do not fit the pattern, then you have found a boundary for generalizing. If you examine instances where your conclusion is not likely to hold and yet it still does hold, then you have reason to expand the boundaries. Testing your pattern in a variety of times, places, situations, and people thus has several advantages over testing in a very narrow range. When you test within a narrow range, even if you do find support for the pattern, this does not help you delineate the boundaries of generalizing.

With a falsification perspective, the goal is *not* to confirm the general claim but rather to alter it to make it less general by eliminating its coverage of instances where it has been found not to hold. Returning to our newscast example, we generalized by situation to include first all television newscasts, then reduced it to all television newscasts in the United States. Let's say all our observations had been on local newscasts up until this point. If so, it would be good to check for patterns in national newscasts. Let's say we watch some national newscasts and again find some inconsistencies with our generalized pattern. In that case, we have found another limit to our general statement, and we must reword the general statement to reflect this limit. At this point, our general statement needs to be amended to read: All *local* television newscasts *in the United States* begin with stories of crime and violence to evoke fear in the audience then make the audience feel good with feature stories and humor. This is still a general statement covering thousands of examples that we never observed, but it is not as general as our first generalized statement. By testing, we have lost some breadth of explanation, but we have gained much in accuracy.

Weeding out the inaccuracies makes for better, although less broad, generalizations. Therefore, the testing process allows you to make better generalizations through falsification. This is significant, because it reduces the number of faulty general claims in your knowledge structures and thus increases your ability to make good decisions.

Heuristic 2: Tentativeness

Remember that you can never fully confirm any inferred statement of a general pattern unless the size of your sample of observations is equal to the size of the population—that is, when you have observed every single element in the entire population to which you want to generalize. Therefore, you need to hold the perspective that your general claims are always tentative. You need to remember that as you continue to test your claim, it is always possible that you could make an observation that will not support your claim. When this occurs, you need to be willing to alter your general claim by shrinking its scope so it no longer includes examples from the observation you made that does not support the full span of the general claim.

Some people feel very uneasy when they are told that the patterns they infer might be wrong and the claims they generalize might be too broad. They don't like being vulnerable to criticisms like these. However, they can take comfort in the fact that this criticism is a two-way street. People who criticize your patterns or generalizations have the burden to back up their criticism with evidence of exceptions to the pattern. If they cannot do this, then their criticism is groundless. If instead they can provide evidence of the limits of your general claim, then you have benefitted from those observations and you have learned something you would not have learned had they not raised their criticism. Remember, if you care about the accuracy of your general claims, then supported criticism is helpful because it shows you how to increase the accuracy of your general claims.

While general claims can rarely be fully supported, there are degrees of support. Just saying that all statements are tentative does not mean that they are all equally valuable or accurate. Some have more support. There is a difference between a haphazardly inferred claim based on only two observations and a carefully inferred claim based on hundreds of observations that find support for it.

III. Avoiding Traps

Induction is almost always used with partially specified problems, so there are many traps that can prevent a person from arriving at an accurate and useful solution. This section provides warnings about five major traps. The first two traps deal with problems that hinder people from noticing patterns. The other three traps deal with generalizing those patterns.

Trap 1: Getting Lost in the Details

Sometimes people get so wrapped up in all the details in each message that they miss seeing the big picture. This happens less with field independent people, but even with those people, there are times when the details seem so overwhelming. When this happens, you need to realize you are too close to the task. Take a break, then come back later with a different perspective that will allow you to see the big picture more clearly and this could make it easier for a pattern to emerge.

Trap 2: Reluctance to Use Intuition

Induction requires the use of some intuition, especially in the early stages when you need to find a pattern across the elements in a set. By *intuition* I do not mean taking a wild guess, which is the way many people define it in everyday language. Instead, I use the definition found in most dictionaries, where **intuition** is defined as the direct perception of truths without any reasoning process. This means that oftentimes you look at the set of elements and you simply "see" the pattern without going through any reasoning process at all. It is as if a light bulb is turned on in your head and you "see" things much more clearly.

This is not to say that reasoning and logic are not important in the inductive process. They are important, but they become much more important after a pattern occurs to you. At that point, you need to think logically about how to make more observations in order to provide a good test of the stability of the pattern you intuited in the initial set of elements. Thus the inductive process values the "jumping to a conclusion" early on, but that is not the end of the process. This conclusion, or claim for a pattern, needs to be tested with more observations.

Although intuition has acquired a pejorative spin (meaning un-scientific, unsystematic, and unsupported claims), it is essential to the inductive process. If you fear taking the leap of inference that enables you to move beyond the limits of providing a literal summary of the examples, you will be stuck in a trap. Take a chance and make a guess. You could be wrong, but if you don't make a tentative guess about a pattern, you will not have the direction to make additional observations to find out if you are wrong. You are stuck. To get unstuck, guess at a pattern. Then you will have some direction when you make more observations and now know better what to look for. If you find evidence of that pattern, your guess was good, so keep making observations. If you do not find evidence of that pattern, then ask yourself what is missing. Look for answers to that question and this will direct you to look for different patterns.

Trap 3: Generalizing Too Far

Generalizing is making a claim that the pattern you perceive in the few observations you made also holds across a much larger set of elements that you did not observe. The temptation is to ask "How far can I go?" and expect a quantitative answer. Rather than think in quantitative terms, think in terms of levels. The examples you observe are limited by time, situation, and people. Each of these concepts is composed of levels. As you move up each level, you are including a larger class of things. For example, let's think about moving up levels of people. Let's say you go visit your friend Sara in her hometown of Savannah, Georgia. When you meet several of her friends, you observe that those people are very sociable and friendly. So you conclude that Sara's hometown friends are all very sociable and friendly. You have not met all of Sara's hometown friends; you have only met a few. On the basis of those few observations, you have generalized to a class of people (all of Sara's hometown friends). Let's call this a level 1 generalization, because you have observed a pattern in a *few* of Sara's friends and moved up one level to *all* of Sara's friends. A level 2 generalization would be to say that all people in Savannah are sociable and friendly; this would include all of Sara's hometown friends plus many more people. A level 3 generalization would claim that all people in Georgia are sociable and friendly; this would also include all the people in Savannah, which also includes all of Sara's hometown friends.

How many levels should you generalize? When generalizing, it is more conservative to move up only one level; that is, a generalization to one higher level is easier for people to accept and for you to defend than is a generalization that moves up several levels. Going up a second level opens you to a barrage of questions: *How do you know all people in Savannah are sociable and friendly when you have only met a few of Sara's hometown friends? What about people Sara does not know? How do you know that they are sociable and friendly?* This is a valid point. How do you know? You have no evidence. So it is better to gather at least some evidence to represent that level of people. Generalize up one level at a time, then gather evidence at that more general level to support that generalization. Then move up one more level, and gather evidence at that level, and so on.

The more you generalize, the shakier is the ground you have to stand on to defend your generalizations. To illustrate this, let's return to our example with Sara. Let's say that during your visit with Sara, you met four of her dozen friends, so your generalization about all her friends is based on about a one-third exposure to her friends. Now let's say you make six more observations, noticing that waitresses in restaurants, clerks in stores, and people on the street are very sociable and friendly. From these 10 observations (four of Sara's friends and six around town), you conclude that all people in Savannah, Georgia are sociable and friendly. This is a class of people that includes Sara's friends but is much larger, about half a million people. Now, let's say you take some day trips and visit some tourist spots around the state of Georgia and during those trips you notice that people are sociable and friendly from 20 observations. So you conclude that all people in Georgia are sociable and friendly. This is a class of people that includes all people in Savannah, which also includes all Sara's friends. You have now moved up to an even higher level of people and this level includes many more people, perhaps 5 million. While you are gathering more observations from a wider group of people, the ratio of the number of observations to the number of people to whom you are generalizing is going down—way down. So while your generalizations are

still based on some evidence, the proportion of that evidence to your speculation is becoming very small indeed.

With induction, you end up walking a very thin line with a big trap on
either side of you. On one side is the trap of overgeneralizing, so that your
conclusion looks like wild speculation that you cannot possibly defend when
challenged. The only thing you can do to avoid this trap is to try to make
as many observations as possible and make sure they are not clustered too
much in one level (with only one type of person, one type of situation, or one
time). On the other side of the thin line is the trap of refusing to generalize at
all. This trap dooms you to treat every observation as unique, so that you are
unwilling to regard similarities across elements as important enough to conclude there is a pattern. You then are in danger of living life in the particulars
and lose sight of the big picture.

There *are* differences across people; we are all individuals. However,
there are also similarities. If you are unwilling to consider the similarities
you observe as being patterns that are worthy of generalization, then you
cannot proceed with the skill of induction. Recognition of patterns across
elements we observe helps us understand much better the nature of things,
helps us predict what will happen, and helps us explain where we fit in the
larger world.

Trap 4: Narrow Base of Observations

Sometimes people will generalize from only one observation (or a very
small set of observations). In this trap, people focus on an isolated incident
and conclude that it represents the typical. For example, people who read a
news story about a criminal who copies an unusual bank robbery depicted in
a popular recent video might conclude that all videos are bad because they
are responsible for the high rate of crime in society. Concluding that all videos are bad because one person copies a particular action in one video is a
faulty general claim. No one video can represent the incredible variety of all
videos. Also, concluding that videos alone are responsible for crime in society
is a faulty induction, because this conclusion fails to consider the many factors that can lead a person to commit a crime.

This induction trap is also frequently in evidence when we try to assess
risk in our personal lives. Often the media will present a story—either as news
or fiction—of an airplane mishap, a stalker, or something that makes us fear-
ful. We then use this one portrayal to overestimate the risk to ourselves from
this type of occurrence while ignoring other things (that the media do not talk
about) that may pose a much higher risk to us. For example, in 1987 many
news reports told about the danger of asbestos in older school buildings and
the risk to children. Fear spread as people induced a belief that all schools had
problems and that their children were at risk. Almost overnight the asbestos
removal industry more than doubled its revenue. However, the actual risk of
a premature death from exposure to asbestos is 1 in 100,000. Compare this to

the rate of premature death due to being struck by lightning at 3 in 100,000. There is also a generalized belief by many in the population that exposure to x-rays in dental and medical offices is risky. It does present a small risk, but the risk of premature death due to smoking cigarettes is 2,920 *times* greater than premature death due to exposure to diagnostic x-rays (Matthews, 1992). However, many people believe that smoking is only a minor risk to their health, while a dentist x-raying their teeth once a year is a major risk.

Trap 5: Faulty Base for Generalizing

Another trap is to infer a pattern from observations of X, then make a general claim that holds for not just X but also Y. For example, sometimes people will make careful observations about how characters in Hollywood videos find romantic partners and how those characters build relationships. They see clear patterns that they use to create beliefs (general claims) about how successful people generate and build romantic relationships. But then they will use these beliefs to guide their behavior in their real lives. This is faulty because they developed the belief from observing one class of elements (characters in Hollywood videos) and generalized it to a belief that it applied to another class of elements (real people in everyday life).

IV. Chapter Review

- The process of induction begins with observations of particular elements in media messages. You need to use your intuition to perceive patterns across those elements and be willing to infer conclusions, knowing that some of them may be wrong. Then once you have inferred a tentative pattern, you need to be willing to continue making observations to test the accuracy of the pattern. As additional observations are found to support the pattern, you have increasing confidence that the pattern can be generalized to all elements in the class of elements you have been observing; that is, you have confidence that you can generalize from your sample of observations to all elements in your population of interest.

- Inferred patterns should always be regarded as being tentative explanations. Someone could always come along later and find an example that does not fit the pattern. However, such nonconfirming examples are valuable in their own way, because they can be used to reformulate the pattern or clarify the extent to which a pattern can be generalized.

- There are also several heuristics that are needed as guidelines to do a good induction. These heuristics provide help to use the power of falsification and to adapt to tentativeness. Finally, it is important to avoid traps, particularly getting lost in details, reluctance to use intuition, generalizing too far, using a narrow base of observations, and relying on a faulty base for generalizing.

Exercise 6.1 Practice Using the Induction Algorithm

This is a sequence of three challenges designed to increase your understanding of using your skill of inducing. This sequence starts with the easiest challenges by providing you with the maximum degree of guidance. As you progress through this sequence, you will find the exercises increasingly challenging because you will have to do more of the thinking for yourself.

Challenge I

1. *Formulate a Question*: Start with asking yourself if Hispanics are under-represented in entertainment videos. In the United States, Hispanics make up about 12% of the total population, so in order for this ethnic group to be fairly represented in the world of video entertainment, they should be about one character for every eight characters shown.

2. *Determine the Element to Observe*: The portrayed ethnicity of characters in videos is the element that is the focus of this induction process.

3. *Make Observations*: Start watching videos with a bit more concentration than you usually do; that is, pay special attention to the ethnicity of characters. As you watch videos over the next few days, keep a running count in your head (or perhaps you want to make marks on a piece of paper so that you don't lose track of your counts over time).

4. *Infer a Pattern*: You are likely to see a pattern very quickly. That pattern is that Hispanics are about one in eight characters, Hispanics are rarely represented, or Hispanics are heavily represented.

5. *Generalize the Pattern*: Think about whether the pattern you found in your few days of viewing videos reflects all videos. Remember that the key to generalizing is that the observations you made in constructing your initial pattern are representative of the larger aggregate. In this case, if the videos you watched were all from Hispanic apps, video on demand (VOD) services, and cable channels, then you were likely to have observed a very high proportion of characters being portrayed as Hispanic; but this pattern is not likely to be an accurate reflection of character portrayals of all characters in videos.

6. *Continue to Test Your Claim*: Search out a wider range of sources of videos and continue to make observations. For example, if your initial pattern was constructed from your exposure to videos from only one cable television channel, then make observations of videos on other cable television channels or pay-per-view services (such as HBO, Netflix, Prime Video, etc.). As you increase your base of observations, notice whether your initial pattern holds up or whether you need to make adjustments to it.

(Continued)

(Continued)

Challenge II

1. *Formulate a Question:* Start with asking yourself whether women who appear in entertainment videos are portrayed as being as powerful and successful as men are.

2. *Determine the Element to Observe:* The simple part of determining an element to observe is gender—that is, whether the character is male or female. The challenging part of this task is determining what it means to be powerful and successful. Can you observe this simply by noticing their portrayed profession? Or is something else required, such as how they act in social situations? Will you need to observe their body language, how they speak, or something else?

3. *Make Observations:* Start watching videos with a bit more concentration than you usually do. Look for indicators of power and success by using the guidelines you developed for yourself in the previous step. As you watch videos over the next few days, keep a running count in your head (or perhaps you want to make marks on a piece of paper so that you don't lose track of your counts over time).

4. *Infer a Pattern:* You are likely to see a pattern very quickly. That pattern is either that women are portrayed with the same indicators of power and success as are men or that the sexes are portrayed in a different manner.

5. *Generalize the Pattern:* Think about whether the pattern you found in your few days of viewing videos reflects all videos. Remember that the key to generalizing is that the observations you made in constructing your initial pattern are representative of the larger aggregate. In this case, if the videos you watched were all from female-focused apps, VOD services, and cable channels, then you were likely to have observed a very high proportion of female characters being portrayed as powerful and successful; but this pattern is not likely to be an accurate reflection of character portrayals of all characters in videos.

6. *Continue to Test Your Claim:* Search out a wider range of sources of videos and continue to make observations. For example, if your initial pattern was constructed from your exposure to videos from only one cable television channel (such as Lifetime or the Hallmark Channel), then make observations of videos on other cable television channels or pay-per-view services (such as HBO, Netflix, Prime Video, etc.). As you increase your base of observations, notice whether your initial pattern holds up or whether you need to make adjustments to it.

Challenge III

1. *Formulate a Question:* In this exercise, the challenge starts with formulating your own question. Think about something that is bothering you across some kind of media message. Maybe you are concerned about pop-up ads, how certain products are advertised, or something about how people treat you on a social networking site. The list of possible questions is endless, so be creative with posing your question.

2. *Determine the Element to Observe:* Your question will suggest what it is you need to observe. If it is not obvious what you need to observe from the way you have posed your question, then you need to refine your question to make it more specific.

3. *Make Observations:* Start observing media messages that would present the kind of elements that are featured in your question. Also think about the range of media messages that could be observed to answer your question. As you make your initial observations, do not worry about trying to cover the entire range. That will come later.

4. *Infer a Pattern:* After you have made a handful of observations, start thinking about whether a pattern is emerging. Don't be afraid to make wild speculations but when you do, continually check those speculations with your observations so that you move toward constructing a pattern that conforms to all your observations as much as possible.

5. *Generalize the Pattern:* Think about how far you can generalize your pattern. For example, if you made observations on only videos, do you think your patterns would also show up in print or audio messages? Or if you made observations only on entertainment messages, do you think that pattern would apply to advertising and news/informational messages also?

6. *Continue to Test Your Claim:* Search out a wider range of sources of media messages and continue making observations to test the stability of your pattern.

Exercise 6.2 Practicing Induction With Other Media Messages

1. Pick a textbook from one of your courses. Flip through it to see if there are pictures.

   Choose another textbook and see if it contains pictures. Keep making observations in many different kinds of textbooks.

   After having examined about half a dozen texts, do you see a pattern developing? Do all textbooks have pictures? If not, what types of textbooks have pictures?

   • Are texts in introductory courses more likely to have pictures?

   • Are texts used in certain academic departments more likely to have pictures?

   • Do texts with pictures tend to cost more than texts without pictures?

   Using your tentative statement about texts with pictures, keep looking at texts to see if your claim holds up. Look for examples to falsify your claim.

   (Continued)

(Continued)

2. Think of the videos you liked best from Exercise 6.1. Go through your memory and write down the list of those videos.

    Analyze those videos for elements that you particularly liked. Do those same kinds of elements show up in all the videos you like? If so, write a general statement that expresses what you like best in videos.

    Now continue to test this general statement. Think of television shows you like. Does that statement apply to TV shows? If so, expand that statement to apply to not just videos but also TV.

    Continue to test this general statement. Think of novels you have read and liked the most. Does this general statement also apply to print stories? If so, expand that statement to apply to stories.

    Continue to test this general statement. Think of happenings in your real life that you have enjoyed the most. Does that statement about stories apply to what happens to you in real life? If so, expand that statement to apply to all events, including mediated stories as well as real-world happenings.

    Think back on the pattern of expanding the statement. How far were you willing to go with it? If you could not expand it past videos, why? What is it about videos that makes certain stories your favorite when they are on the big screen but not when they are on the small screen (TV)?

3. Go to your favorite source of news. This source can be a daily newspaper, a magazine, a website, a blog, or another source. Pick a day and read through several news stories presented by your selected news source.

    Analyze the news stories for the number of facts each one presents. Also, notice several characteristics about each news story (e.g., the author of each story, the topic of each story, etc.).

    Do you see a pattern? For example, is there a particular author who presents a lot of facts in her news stories compared to other authors? Or perhaps local news stories seem to present more facts than do news stories about national or international topics.

    Now test your initial impression of this pattern by analyzing the news stories across different days presented in your favorite news sources.

    Does your initial speculation about a pattern hold up? Or are there lots of exceptions to your speculation of a pattern? If this is the case, then you will need to alter your perception of a pattern.

    Continue to test the pattern and make alterations when needed.

    As you continue to test your pattern, you will eventually find that your pattern is exhibited over and over without exception (or very, very, few exceptions). At this point, you have found a pattern that is very stable. Remember that you need to avoid claiming that you have "confirmed" the pattern, because you have not tested it on all possible news stories presented by your favorite news source. However, you have achieved the goal of induction, which is to discover patterns that are highly stable.

4. Think about the people who you regard as your closest friends.

    Analyze those friendships for elements that you particularly like. Do those same kinds of elements show up in all your friendships? If so, write a general statement that expresses what you require most in close friendships.

    Now continue to test this general statement. Think of television shows you like. Does that statement apply to TV shows? If so, expand that statement to apply to not just videos but also TV.

    Continue to test this general statement. Think of novels you have read and liked the most. Does this general statement also apply to print stories? If so, expand that statement to apply to stories.

Deducing
Reasoning with Logic from General Principles

Deduction is the skill of using a few premises to reason logically toward a conclusion. The basic procedure of deduction follows a reasoning process in the form of a syllogism, which is a set of three statements. The first statement in the set is called the **major premise**; it is usually a general principle or rule. The second statement is called the **minor premise**; it is usually an observation. The third statement is the reasoned **conclusion**. We use logic to see if the observation fits the rule and then derive the conclusion.

Perhaps the most familiar example of a syllogism is the one that uses the following two premises: (1) All men are mortal and (2) Socrates is a man. From this we can conclude that Socrates is mortal. The first premise is the major one; that is, it states a general proposition. The second premise is the minor one; that is, it provides information about something specific (in this case, a specific person) in a way that relates it to the major premise. Using logic, we see that the observation in the second premise fits the rule in the first premise and we conclude that Socrates is mortal.

Deduction is the skill that the fictional detective Sherlock Holmes employed so successfully to make sense of clues and solve crimes. He knew a great deal about the physical world and about human behavior; this knowledge was his bank of major premises. He had keen powers of observation, so he was able to recognize clues that were the most relevant to solving a crime; his observations were his minor premises. When Sherlock Holmes found a clue (such as a scratch on a walking cane, mud on someone's shoes, or the gardener taking walks in the middle of the night), he had a minor premise (the second statement in his syllogisms). He then searched his knowledge bank for a relevant general principle that could be used to explain the minor premise; this general principle became his major premise (the first statement in his syllogisms). He then used the general principle to explain the clue and this produced a conclusion. To Sherlock Holmes, this process of logical reasoning uses syllogisms. To us readers, he appeared to be a genius in his crime-solving ability but as he often said, "It's elementary!" meaning that this was simple to him. And yes, the process of logical reasoning with a syllogism was easy for Sherlock Holmes; what was difficult was acquiring all the general principles and making good observations.

You use the skill of deduction quite frequently in your everyday life, although you may not have been referring to it as "deduction." For example, you are likely to have a general principle such as "If I work hard in a course, I will do well and earn a high grade" and have used it often. Also, you frequently monitor your study behavior and make observations such as "I have worked hard in this course." With such a major and minor premise, you are likely to conclude with confidence that "I will do well in this course and earn a high grade!" You can easily reason from these particular major and minor premises to this logical conclusion.

At this point, you might be thinking "This is so obvious!" But this is precisely the point—deduction should be obvious. The essence of deduction is to reduce things to a simple logical process where the conclusion seems so obvious that no one would dispute it. Let's take a look at the algorithm that will help you do this.

I. The Deduction Algorithm

Deduction follows three steps: (1) begin with an observation, (2) identify a relevant general principle, and (3) use the two premises and reason to a conclusion (Table 7.1). Let's examine these in detail.

Step 1: Begin With an Observation

You see something happen in your everyday life and wonder why. For example, let's say you get back your first short essay test in a particular course and are shocked to see that you did poorly. You could look at how your answer on each question was graded, but that is likely to give you information at too micro a level; you want to know why you did badly on the test more so than why you did poorly on an individual answer. You might find that you earned few points on one question because you did not provide much evidence to back up your argument. You lost half a point on another question because a definition was missing a key element. You could fix these particulars on this exam and console yourself by thinking that you would not do so poorly if the professor were to grade the exam again. But that does not help you with the next exam, because none of the particular questions on this exam will show up on the next exam. Finding particular examples of where you did not earn more points will not help you do better on the next test *unless* you can find a general principle that applies as an explanation for why you did poorly on this test.

TABLE 7.1	The Skill of Deducing

Purpose: To use general principles to construct a conclusion about an example

Algorithm:

1. Begin with an observation.
2. Identify a relevant general principle.
3. Use the two premises to reason logically to a conclusion.

Step 2: Identify a Relevant General Principle

In this step, you search your **knowledge structures** to find a principle that would provide a rule to interpret the observation. This is the fundamental reason why knowledge structures are so important. When you have many useful knowledge structures, then you can easily find a relevant general principle to explain any observation you may make. For example, people who have highly developed knowledge structures about communication and psychology will be better able to make sense of the relationships they have in their lives. People who have highly developed knowledge structures about economics and business will be better able to make sense of investments and plan for their financial futures.

How do these principles get into our knowledge structures? They come from education. In fact, the primary purpose of education is to provide us with general principles or at least the means to find them or construct them for ourselves. By using the term *education* in this sense, I mean education broadly to include both formal education (in schools) and informal education (self-motivated and self-guided). As for formal education, schools create experiences and challenges to expose you to a wide variety of ideas, that is why all high schools emphasize the need for you to study some form of literature, history, physical science, math, and a language other than your native tongue. The first 2 years at most colleges require you to take something called "distribution requirements," which are courses distributed across the major bodies of knowledge so that you can fill up your knowledge bank with potentially useful information.

Step 3: Use the Two Premises to Reason Logically to a Conclusion

There are two forms of logical reasoning: **classification reasoning** and **linear reasoning**. Which one you choose depends on the nature of the relationship between the two premises.

The Socrates example is a categorical syllogism; that is, it deals with the judgment of whether something belongs in a category or not, so the form of reasoning is classification. In this example, the category is "mortal" and the rule given to us is "All men are mortal." So when our observation of Socrates tells us that he is a man, we know that we can apply the general premise and must decide whether to put him in the category of "mortal" or "immortal." The rule tells us that we must put him in the mortal category. If we observe Socrates to be a dog, then the general premise does not apply and we must look for another general premise.

Let's return to the example begun in Step 1 above. This too requires classification. You observe that you did poorly on an exam. You search your experience and locate the general principle: If I do not study enough, I will do poorly on an exam. Applying that rule along with your observation, you logically must conclude that you did not study enough.

In contrast to classification reasoning, we have linear reasoning. With linear reasoning we again start with two premises and reason to a third, but in this case we cannot identify one of the premises as being major and one as minor—or one as general and one as particular. Instead both premises operate at the same level of importance or generality; that is, they are both general principles or they are both observations.

The key to linear reasoning is to focus on associations among the elements in the two premises. Let's look at the following example: (1) Larry is smarter than Curly and (2) Moe is smarter than Larry. Who is the smartest of the three? The answer of course is Moe. This conclusion is easy to reach when the two premises are stated clearly and in parallel form.

When the two premises are not stated in parallel form—such as when one is positive and one is negative—more effort is required in the reasoning process. To illustrate: (1) Sally is not as smart as Ellen and (2) Sally is smarter than Harry. Who is the smartest? The answer is Ellen, but this requires a bit more mental effort in the reasoning process. Let's try one more example: (1) Professor Alplanap is a much harder grader than Professor Bootreau and (2) Professor Cawleeni is a much easier grader than Professor Bootreau. We compare the three people in the two statements in terms of difficulty as a grader and must conclude the following: (3) Therefore, Professor Alplanap is a harder grader than Professor Cawleeni.

II. Heuristics

What's the big deal? Why do we need an entire chapter on something so simple and logical? The simplicity is deceptive. Of course we want to set up our deduction problems so that there is a clear pair of statements that gives us the ability to use classification or linear reasoning to arrive at what should be a clear and airtight conclusion that everyone would accept. However, the world rarely gives us such a neat problem because most problems are not fully specified.

To this point in the chapter, I have greatly simplified the process of deduction so that you can understand its essence and become comfortable with it. Now it is time to uncover some of the more prevalent challenges. I will present some of these in this section on the **probability premise heuristic** and the **conditional reasoning heuristic**, and I will discuss others in the next section on traps.

Heuristic 1: Probability Premise

Sometimes we might use a premise that is not absolute. Here's an example: "Most people who live in San Francisco are Democrats." Let's say we meet Sally and find out she lives in San Francisco. If we use the major premise and we forget the adjective "most," thus treating the premise as an absolute general rule, we will conclude that Sally must be a Democrat. This of course is a mistake. Sally could be a Republican, an Independent, or many other non-Democrat things.

Frequently the major premises we use are not absolute; that is, they allow for exceptions. When a proposition uses words such as "many," "most," or "almost all," they appear as a general rule but they are allowing for exceptions. In essence, they are saying that the rule is likely to hold but not always. Thus we refer to these as probabilistic statements; that is, if you follow the rule in your reasoning process, you are likely to be right—the probability is on your side. However, you could be wrong.

If our goal in reasoning is efficiency, then probabilistic statements are not a problem. Probabilistic statements are better than nothing; they help us reduce uncertainty even though there are times that our conclusions can be wrong. In everyday life, many of our conclusions have trivial consequences so being wrong is not disastrous. Or we often have chances to correct our conclusions. For example, if we are having a conversation with Sally after we first meet her, we might make a wrong conclusion but could correct it very quickly.

However, if we are trying to reason toward a conclusion that will have major consequences, we need to reject the goal of efficiency and replace it with the goal of accuracy. In this case, probabilistic statements can pose serious problems, so it is important to try to find an absolute statement to replace a probabilistic statement. When it is not possible to find an absolute statement (and this is often the case), then you need to determine what the level of probability is in your probabilistic statement. Not all levels of probability are the same. Some levels are very high and can provide almost as much assurance as an absolute statement. For example, the term "most" in a probabilistic statement could mean 51% or 99%, which makes a huge difference in the level of confidence we will have in our conclusions based on the major premise. We should seek out percentages to make the major premises more precise. Then when we arrive at our conclusion and express it, we should include the percentage as a probability level for the confidence we have in our conclusion. Returning to the example of Sally, if we knew that 70% of all the registered voters in San Francisco were Democrats and we knew that Sally was registered to vote in San Francisco, we could conclude that there is a 70% probability that Sally is a Democrat.

Scientists report probability values for their conclusions. That is part of their training as scientists. If you are in the physical or social sciences, then you frequently see conclusions with P-values (probability values). If you are in the humanities or the arts, you rarely see things quantified like this. However, there are times when it would be useful to have some quantities. For example, let's say you have an assignment to do a term paper. It would help if you knew what the probability of earning an A was if you put 10 hours of work into the paper. What if you put 50 hours of work into it? If you knew these probabilities and they were accurate, you could plan to use your time in the most efficient manner to achieve your goals.

There are times in our lives when it is very important to have precise probabilities in our major premise when making our decisions. For example, let's say you were considering laser surgery on your eyes to correct your vision and the doctor told you that "most" people see much better after the laser surgery and the rest go blind. You would certainly want to know what she meant by "most." Would you have the surgery if your doctor said that "most" meant 54%? What if she said that "most" meant 99.999%? When there are major consequences to your deduced conclusions, you need to have precise and accurate probability figures in your major premise.

Heuristic 2: Conditional Reasoning

Not all syllogisms follow a categorical or linear reasoning process. Some follow a conditional reasoning process. Conditional reasoning relies on conditions that underlie the logic rather than categories. Here is an example of conditional reasoning: (1) If Harry misses any of his math classes, he will not pass his mid-term exam. (2) Harry passed his mid-term exam. (3) Therefore, Harry did not miss any of his math classes. This syllogism uses (1) as the major premise; this is the condition. Harry passed his mid-term exam because this condition was met. So far, so good. But what if Harry failed his mid-term exam? In this case, can we say that he must have missed some of his math classes? The answer is no, because there could be other conditions required for passing and these other conditions are not presented in the major premise. In other words, going to class is not a sufficient condition to pass the mid-term—that is, this one condition by itself is not enough to ensure Harry's success. Let's say that passing an exam is based on three conditions: (1) Harry must attend all classes before the exam, (2) Harry must study for at least 20 hours, and (3) Harry must have a tutor explain things to him outside of class. If all three of these conditions are necessary, then Harry must meet all three conditions in order to pass. Conforming to only one or even two of them is not good enough to avoid failure. Therefore, to avoid this type of trap in reasoning, we must ensure that our major premise includes either (a) a sufficient condition or (b) the full set of necessary conditions.

Conditional reasoning can also incorporate probabilistic statements. For example, let's say you are in a psychology course where the professor gives 10 weekly quizzes, each worth 10 points. At the end of the quarter, the professor sums all the points you earned and assigns you a grade based on the traditional grading scale: 90 to 100 is an A, 80 to 89 is a B, 70 to 79 is a C, 60 to 69 is a D, and below 60 points is an F. Let's say that you earn a 10 on each of the first two quizzes. Can you assess the probability that you will receive an A in the course? We all try to do this, and when we do, we would say our chances are very high. But this is only a guess. We could say 100% probability, or we could say 90% probability—neither of these guesses is more accurate because we don't have enough information to assess an accurate probability. Instead our estimate of probability is based only on optimism. In contrast, let's say that we earn only a 3 on the first quiz and a 6 on the second quiz. We have enough information to compute the probability of earning an A as zero, because even if we earn the full 10 on all of the remaining eight quizzes, our total will only sum to 89 and that is not enough points to be in the A range.

III. Avoiding Traps

In this section, I will focus on six major traps that are dangers when using the skill of deduction. The first three traps are alerts in dealing with the major premise. This is the starting place for the reasoning process. If the starting place is faulty, irrelevant, or too complex, then the reasoning process will not lead to a useful conclusion.

Trap 1: Faulty Major Premise

We must begin with a major premise that is accurate. Let's return to the Socrates syllogism. If we began with the premise of "All men live forever" instead of "All men are mortal," then we would have the following:

All men live forever.

Socrates is a man.

Therefore, Socrates will live forever.

This is a very simple example. Its simplicity makes it a good illustration of a faulty major premise and how it can invalidate the conclusion. If you start with a faulty major premise, it does not matter how well you reason to a conclusion because your conclusion will always be wrong.

In our everyday lives, we often use faulty premises. We may have incorporated wrong information into our knowledge structures and this has resulted in a faulty general principle residing there. Or perhaps the general principle was valid when we incorporated it into our knowledge structure, but things have changed and we have not yet updated and altered the principle to maintain its accuracy.

Trap 2: Irrelevant Major Premise

It is a trap to start with a major premise that does not express a good classification rule for the ideas in the minor premise. The major premise itself might be clear and it might be a good rule in many circumstances, but it is being used in a faulty manner if it does not express a good classification rule *for your particular purposes*. For example, let's alter our Socrates syllogism a bit to read as follows: (1) All men are mortal and (2) Socrates is not a man (he's my dog!). If we mistakenly force the major premise to be used to classify the mortality of Socrates, we would conclude that Socrates is not mortal by using the following reasoning process: (1) Because Socrates is NOT a man and (2) because all men are mortal, (3) therefore Socrates must NOT be mortal. By using the wrong general premise, we are stuck in a bad place. We could go back and look for a better major premise, such as "All living things are mortal," and this would set up a better process of deduction where we would conclude that Socrates is mortal, even though he is a dog and not a man. But many people do not want to expend the mental effort to think carefully about the appropriateness of their major premise; they would rather use what they already have to force a conclusion. This is more efficient, and efficiency is often more important to people than is accuracy.

Let's consider another example of this trap, one where the flaw in using the wrong major premise is not as obvious as with the Socrates dog example. Let's say you read the results of a research study that says that the most intelligent people of the past several generations have chosen careers in science rather than in politics. You use this as a major premise when you consider the intelligence of our current president and conclude that he is not very smart. This conclusion is easy to arrive at and one that many people have reasoned. But let's look more carefully at the major premise. It really claims that the most intelligent people do not go into politics, but it does not say that all intelligent people avoid politics. Perhaps those with IQs above 130 all go into science rather than politics—these are the most intelligent ones. The major premise then would say nothing about people with IQs of 130 or below. Let's say our president has an IQ of 125—that would place him in the top 1% of the population as far as IQ. He would not be as smart as the geniuses, but he would be smarter than 99% of the population.

Trap 3: Too Complex a Major Premise Is Needed

Sometimes a simple syllogistic reasoning process is too simple for arriving at a good conclusion. Either that or the major premise needs to be far more complex; this is the case when there are multiple causes for an event and when none of those causes are sufficient or even necessary. For example, we all accept the principle that you need to study in order to do well on an exam. That is the major premise in the following simple syllogism:

In order to do well on an exam, Sara must study.

Sara studied.

Therefore, Sara will do well on the exam.

But perhaps Sara studied and did NOT do well on the exam. Perhaps Sara studied the wrong material. Perhaps Sara did not study enough. We know from experience that studying by itself does not guarantee success on an exam, so we need to incorporate more information into our major premise because studying is not a sufficient cause of success on a test. To complicate things further, we must consider that studying may not even be a necessary condition. Some students can do well on a test without studying for it. These students have one or more other factors that could explain test success. Some examples of these factors are as follows: the student already had a great deal of background knowledge on a topic; the student attended all class lectures, concentrated during class, and absorbed the information without the need to study outside of class; or perhaps the exam was relatively easy.

When we need to reason well to a conclusion that has great importance to us, we need to examine the major premise carefully to determine whether it is okay to keep it simple or whether it needs to include more than one condition. Then when you are considering a major premise that requires multiple conditions, ask yourself if all of those conditions are necessary. The simplest major premise expresses one and only one sufficient condition, such that if the condition is met in our observation expressed in the minor premise, then we can safely and accurately reason to the conclusion.

Trap 4: Conditional Reasoning

Conditional reasoning offers a special kind of trap. This trap focuses on the direction of the relationship between the major premise and the minor premise. For example, consider the following two premises: (1) If Harry misses any math classes, he will not pass the mid-term. (2) Harry did not miss any math classes. Can we conclude that Harry passed his mid-term? The answer is no, because the premise only says that missing class will lead to failure; it says nothing about his attendance leading to passing the mid-term. Here the relationship is not symmetrical; that is, the relationship flows only one way. Missing a math class will guarantee a failure, but attending all math classes will not guarantee a pass. In short, missing a math class is a sufficient condition for failure, but attending all math classes is only a necessary condition for a pass. To guarantee a pass, Harry must go to all classes but he must also meet some other necessary conditions.

Trap 5: Irrational Reasoning

There are times when we may not let ourselves use rational reasoning. At times like these, we are often emotional and cannot get around the emotions to see things more clearly. Or if we do see things clearly, we still cannot make ourselves behave in a rational manner. For example, there are many people who have seen *Jaws* and some of the film's images scared them so badly that they immediately constructed the general rule of "If I go in the water, I will put myself at high risk for being attacked by a shark." When these people envision themselves in the water, they feel fear because they associate this with a shark attack. This happens with many people even when they are swimming in a lake; although the swimmers know that sharks are salt water creatures and are not found in fresh water lakes, their fear is so great that they cannot allow themselves to reason rationally. With some people, the general principle is so strong that they apply it even when they are swimming in a backyard pool. There are many other examples of how the emotion of fear (or any other emotion) leads people to reason irrationally from general principles and thus greatly overestimate (or underestimate) their risk in many situations. For example, some people want to avoid contamination from dental x-rays during regular checkups at the dentist, yet they willingly tolerate the risk from smoking cigarettes. Even if these people were to get a tooth x-ray every time they smoked a cigarette, their risk from premature death would still be far greater from smoking than from the x-rays.

Another example is with emotions, such as love or lust. We all have dating rules for ourselves, such as "I will not date someone who has X," where X could be a history of bad behavior, someone who has hurt you before, someone who your parents like, someone who has served time in prison more than once, and so on. Then you meet Chris who has X. Logically you must conclude from your rule that you should not date Chris. However, there is something that really attracts you to Chris and you begin dating.

Trap 6: Unwillingness to Build Knowledge Structures

Perhaps the biggest trap of all is to avoid opportunities to build knowledge structures on new topics. In essence, the college experience is the 4-year opportunity to expose yourself to many different bodies of knowledge so that you can construct a wide variety of knowledge structures as a strong foundation for any kind of career. However, the irony in higher education is that most students regard this opportunity for breadth as something to be avoided so they can instead pursue a much narrower set of courses that will prepare them for an entry-level job in a career they think they would like, although they have no direct experience in that type of career. Thus, many students think it a waste of 4 years to explore a wide range of experiences before locking themselves into a choice of a 40-year-plus career path.

In order to avoid this common trap, you need to change your perspective on college. Shift away from viewing a college education as a technical school that will train you for a particular job, and instead think of a college education as an opportunity to expand your mind and obtain a set of knowledge structures across a broad range of topics. College does this in two ways. One way is to show us a wide range of general principles. Professors are experts in their particular fields, so they can show you the most important things within their field. But their expertise is typically narrow, so you cannot depend on any one professor to teach you everything. You need to seek out experts in a wide range of fields. And even more importantly, you need to learn how to apply the skills well as outlined in this book so that you can continually add to your knowledge structures and update them on your own. General principles are constantly changing.

IV. Chapter Review

- The skill of deduction can be applied easily in very simple situations. However, there are far more complex situations than there are simple situations, because the world is complex, constantly changing, and continually presenting us with partially specified problems. The key to deducing well is to cut through the complexity of problems to find their central essence as expressed in a general premise and a particular premise. This will allow you to proceed efficiently to an accurate conclusion.

- As you develop your skill of deduction, you will find that the greatest challenge lies less in knowing how to reason logically to conclusions and more with knowing how to select accurate and useful general principles. When you start with a faulty general premise, you are guaranteed to arrive at a faulty conclusion. It is important to be accurate with your decisions, especially with decisions that will have a significant influence on your life. In order to achieve greater accuracy, you need to be very careful in identifying a general premise and clearly understand the relationship between the major and the minor premises. Finally, to make your reasoning more precise, be clear about whether the reasoning requires a categorical, conditional, or linear judgment.

- Many scholars treat deductive reasoning as the strongest part of human thought, the epitome of rationality, and the foundation of logic (Copi, 1978; McCawley, 1981; Quine, 1972). But this type of thought emulates a computer—systematic, logical, and rational—following the prescribed algorithms. There are others who acknowledge that humans get into trouble with the deductive thinking process when problems they address are partially specified; that is, they are missing important bits of information and therefore the application of a computer-like algorithm breaks down. However, unlike computers, humans are able to muddle through in such instances.

- This is one of the wonderful things about being human. When we don't have enough information to solve a problem and cannot set up a deductive process, we go outside the problem to get what we need. In this way we are very different from computers. The more we learn about how the brain functions, the more we come to realize that the brain is not a logical computer. In his book, *How the Mind Works*, Steven Pinker (1997) contrasts human brains with computers, saying "computers are serial, doing one thing at a time; brains are parallel, doing millions of things at once. Computers are fast; brains are slow. Computer parts are reliable; brain parts are noisy. Computers have a limited number of connections; brains have trillions. Computers are assembled according to a blueprint; brains must assemble themselves" (p. 26). This does not mean that computers are superior to the human brain. In some ways, the human brain is far superior to any computer. There are things the human brain can do that computers cannot do. We as humans are comfortable solving partially specified problems, while a computer will freeze when faced with such a problem.

Exercise 7.1 Practice Using the Deducing Algorithm

This is a sequence of three challenges designed to increase your understanding of using your skill of deducing. This sequence starts with the easiest challenges by providing you with the maximum degree of guidance. As you progress through this sequence, you will find the exercises increasingly challenging because you will have to do more of the thinking for yourself.

Challenge I

1. *Make an Observation:* Observe something in an entertainment-type message.

2. *Identify a Relevant General Principle:* Use the following statement as a general proposition: All entertainment messages are designed to trigger wanted emotional reactions.

3. *Reason to a Conclusion:* Can you use the general principle to explain the nature of the observation you made?

Challenge II

1. *Make an Observation:* Observe something in an advertising-type message.

2. *Identify a Relevant General Principle:* Use the following statement as a general proposition: All advertising messages are designed to convince you that you have a need and that the advertised product/service can satisfy your need.

3. *Reason to a Conclusion:* Can you use the general principle to explain the nature of the observation you made?

Challenge III

1. *Make an Observation:* Observe something in any kind of a media message.

2. *Identify a Relevant General Principle:* Can you think of a general principle that would explain the observation you just made?

3. *Reason to a Conclusion:* Can you use the general principle to explain the nature of the observation you made?

Exercise 7.2 More Exercises for Deducing

1. Check the following major premises for accuracy. Which of these premises are faulty?

   A. All people from Alabama have Southern accents.

   B. All welfare recipients are ethnic minorities.

   C. All days end in darkness.

   D. All medical doctors are competent.

   E. All college professors have earned a PhD degree.

   F. All dogs are mammals.

2. Consider the following syllogism:

   > Successful students study hard.

   > Harry works hard.

   Can we conclude that therefore Harry is successful? Is the major premise relevant to the minor premise; that is, is working hard and studying hard the same thing?

3. *Symmetry:* Consider the following syllogisms and decide which are faulty because of symmetrical reasoning. It might be helpful to draw a Venn diagram to help you "see" the relationships.

   > Healthy people work out every day.
   > Harry is healthy.
   > Harry works out every day.

   > Some criminals are in jail.
   > No blondes are criminals.
   > There are no blondes in jail.

   > All cats have nine lives.
   > Cats are mammals.
   > Mammals have nine lives.

4. *Linear Ordering:* Consider the following sets of statements. For each set, decide whether the last statement can be deduced from the other statements, and if so, whether it is accurate.

   > The chair is to the left of the table.
   > The lamp is to the right of the table.
   > The lamp is to the right of the chair.

   > Molly is a faster runner than Brianna.
   > Brianna is a slower runner than Daisy.
   > Molly is a faster runner than Sarah.
   > Daisy is a faster runner than Molly.

Synthesizing

Assembling Novel Configurations

Synthesis is the assembling of individual elements into a coherent whole. The "whole" can be many different things such as a knowledge structure, an opinion on a controversial issue, a solution to a problem, or an original message. With synthesis, the "whole" is something new; that is, synthesis is not taking something apart then simply putting it back together. For example, if you take apart a complicated machine then put all the parts back together, that is not synthesis; that is reassembly. But if you take apart a machine, throw out the parts that do not work well, replace those parts with new components, then put all the pieces (new and old) back together so that the machine runs better than it did before, that is synthesis.

With media literacy, of course, we are not concerned with taking apart machines or other tangible devices. Instead, we are concerned with taking apart either media messages or the opinions, beliefs, and sets of knowledge we have residing in our own minds.

Among the set of seven media literacy skills highlighted in this book, synthesis is the most complicated because it incorporates the use of other skills in its process, especially the skills of analysis, evaluation, and grouping. Also, applying the skill of synthesis involves both sides of the brain. The left side is needed for systematic reasoning and the right side is needed for creativity. Both sides need to work together in a balanced manner. If the left side dominates, then the synthesis will look too much like a relatively simple reassembly of old elements. If the right side dominates, then the synthesis will result in something novel but it might not work as well (or at all) so the product of all that effort will end up having no utility.

I. Challenges

Like with the other media literacy skills, synthesis can be conducted over a range of challenges. I begin this chapter by focusing your attention on two types of challenges that require the application of the skill of synthesis—the **alteration challenge** and the **creation challenge**. Although both of these challenges involve the tasks of altering and creating, the alteration type of synthesis is focused much more on fixing some existing set of ideas and information to make it function better, so the challenge is to make alterations to accomplish the fixing. In contrast, the creation challenge is focused much more on constructing something new that breaks with the past and generates a fresh perspective.

Challenge 1: Alteration

Oftentimes people will become uncomfortable with an existing knowledge structure. They may feel that the knowledge structure contains a good deal of information that is outdated, or they may be encountering a significant amount of information that runs counter to the information in their existing knowledge structure. For example, let's say you hold a particular belief on a controversial issue but lately you have been encountering information that refutes some of the facts that you use to support your existing belief. You start feeling an increasing degree of dissonance and this is motivating you to do something about your existing belief. So you begin checking facts and find that some of the facts supporting your belief are still accurate but others are outdated or have been found to be faulty. Also, you find that some of the newer information you are encountering is accurate but some of it is faulty. So you conduct a synthesis to weed out the faulty facts, look for additional facts, then assemble all these selected elements into a new belief that is a coherent whole. Your new belief is not radically different from your old one; instead it is an alteration that accommodates new information in place of faulty information.

Challenge 2: Creation

A second type of challenge that requires use of the skill of synthesis is the creation of something novel. For example, let's say that you have been struggling with a problem that has arisen in your relationship with someone very important to you, such as your partner. You have tried different things to try to solve the problem but nothing has worked. So you decide to engage in a synthesis to create a new strategy to solve your problem. You begin with the big picture by analyzing your relationship and identify all the things you like and do not like about your partner and your relationship. Then you analyze all the strategies you have tried in the past to solve the problem, and you evaluate the elements in those many strategies. Some of those elements have worked to varying degrees but others have not. So you disregard the elements that have not worked and bring forward all the elements that had some value in the past. This results in a lot of elements that you could simply list, but listing elements is not the same as creating a new strategy. So instead of listing those elements, you group them in some way. You could group by effectiveness, putting the elements that have worked best into one group and then creating other groups for elements that worked okay and those that worked a little. But that kind of grouping is not likely to move you closer to creating a strategy. Another way might be to group by situation. You notice that some of the elements have worked when you were in public, other elements worked best when you were in small groups with friends, and other elements worked best when you were alone with your partner. This grouping is better than simply listing the elements because it gives you insights about how to act differently across situations, but perhaps there is an even better way to group that would deliver even more insights into how to strengthen your relationship. So you think about grouping on your partner's needs and you create groups for the needs of intimacy, honesty, excitement, and affection. You then sort the elements into these groups. If you rank order these groups in terms of how important each need is to your partner, then you are moving toward a strategy that shows you which elements you should use first and which other elements also should be used but in more of a secondary way. As you can see in this example, applying the skill of synthesis requires a process that involves the systematic application of other skills (analysis, evaluation, and grouping). It also involves the application of creative insights, such as determining which analytical dimensions to use in the analysis, selecting which standards to use in the evaluation, and playing around with various grouping schemes that will help you move closer to perceiving the essence of your relationship with your partner and thereby understanding the key factors needed to construct a better relationship.

As you can see from these descriptions, applying the skill of synthesis is more involved that applying the other skills highlighted in this book. Now let's take a closer look at the process of applying this skill.

II. The Synthesis Algorithm

The *process* of synthesis is presented below in four steps (Table 8.1). Although the actual use of the skill of synthesis appears in step 4, the first three steps are essential to the process. Without the first three steps, the synthesis itself will not have what it needs to be successful. These first three steps may take weeks or months if you are working on a major problem and do a systematic and thorough job. However, these first three steps can be completed in a manner of seconds if you cut corners, rely on intuition, and are more interested in efficiency more than effectiveness.

Step 1: Determine Your Purpose

The first step is to determine your purpose for the synthesis. Usually the purpose is to address some sort of a problem that has captured your interest. Perhaps you have noticed a problem with a belief you hold; lately you have been encountering information that does not support your belief, so you have a problem to determine whether you should hold onto your belief or alter it in some way. Perhaps you are faced with a major decision, such as what kind of career to pursue, whether to take a relationship to the next level or to get out of it, or whether to make an expensive purchase or not. If it is a major problem, you have likely been thinking about the problem for a long time and even mulled it over with friends, but nothing you come up with seems good enough as a solution. Or perhaps you have been bothered by something but can't figure out what is really bothering

TABLE 8.1	The Skill of Synthesizing

Purpose: To assemble elements into a new structure

Algorithm:

1. Determine your purpose for the synthesis.

2. Gather information.

3. Filter for acceptable elements by selecting the elements in a process of evaluation.

   o Discard the elements that are found unacceptable due to their not meeting a standard (such as accuracy, utility, etc.).
   o Keep the elements that are found to be acceptable.

4. Assemble the selected elements into a coherent whole.

   o If the whole is complete (attains your goal), you have finished the synthesis.
   o If the whole is not complete, select and/or create additional elements that will fill the gaps and complete the whole.

you. The problem appears too large, too amorphous, too complex, or too dynamic, and you can't get a handle on it. These are all good purposes for conducting a synthesis.

Step 2: Gather Information

The second step in the synthesis is to gather information on the topic of the problem. For example, let's say your problem is that you cannot select a career path. In this case, think about what you know about different careers. Maybe you have gotten some of this information from people you know who work in different careers; however, the breadth of this information would be limited. You also have some information about various careers from the media, such as watching characters in fictional movies and videos portraying different careers such as doctors, lawyers, detectives, forensic scientists, politicians, advertisers, athletes, musicians, and spies.

Step 2 requires the use of the skill of analysis. Do a component analysis to make sure you have information on the key factors of careers, such as the training required, types of duties and tasks, compensation, and lifestyle. These become your analytical dimensions. Do an outline analysis to help organize the information gathered in a simple component analysis. This may require you to read through masses of words on websites and books, so you need to conduct an analysis to find the key bits of information you need.

This step also engages the skill of grouping. As you collect your information, put those informational elements into groups. The most obvious way of doing this on the task of deciding on a career is to create a category for each career. As each group fills with information, you will be guided to direct your effort most efficiently by shifting your attention to groups with the smallest amount of information.

Step 3: Filter for Acceptable Elements

After you have gathered a great deal of information, the next step is to sort through all the informational elements to filter in the acceptable elements and filter out the unacceptable ones. This requires using the skill of evaluation, in which the informational elements are compared to a standard. In this evaluation, the standards would be relevance and accuracy. First, you want to make sure that the information is relevant to your problem. That is, have you gathered information on professions that you have no intention of pursuing? If so, screen out this information. Have you collected facts that are too peripheral to your decision about a career path? If so, then screen out this information. Second, you want to make sure that the information you have gathered is accurate. That is, are there places where one informational element contradicts another informational element? If so, you need to determine which one is accurate and filter out the rest as being faulty.

When you have finished these two steps, you have a group of relevant and accurate informational elements for each career you are considering. The next step is to rank order the informational elements in each group according to how attractive they are to you. For example, in one group, the compensation may be ranked first because the pay is high but the actual work tasks might be ranked low because they appear very boring to you. In another group, the lifestyle might be ranked high while the training is ranked low.

Up to this point, the left side of your brain dominates the task. The more complete and the more systematic you are with the analysis, grouping, and evaluation, the better your base of raw material. This is not the synthesis itself, but it is the essential prelude to it. Without this preparation, the raw materials are gathered in an intuitive manner almost "on the fly" as you think up the pieces as you need them to build your synthesis.

You can stop the process at this point and simply make a selection of one career by choosing the career in the group that has the largest collection of filtered informational elements or the group that has the most highly ranked informational elements. If you do make a selection at this point, then the process has been determined primarily by the skill of evaluation, not synthesis. But let's say that you cannot see an obvious winner from the groupings you have made; that is, each group has elements you like in a career but each group also has elements you do not like. You do not see a career that is attractive enough (lots of positive elements and few or no negative elements) for you to select it and reject the rest with confidence. In this case, you will likely ask yourself, "Can I use this information to construct a vision of the best career for me?" This question will motivate you to move to the next step, where you will use synthesis to answer this question.

Step 4: Assemble the Selected Elements Into a Coherent Whole

The fourth step in this process is to apply the skill of synthesis, which is assembling the elements from your preparation into a meaningful whole. In our example, this meaningful whole would be a detailed articulation of a career that would best fit your needs, abilities, and expectations for a life's work. This articulation does not exist in any one of your career groups that you fashioned up to this point, so you must construct this ideal grouping of characteristics. Synthesis is the skill you can use as a tool to accomplish this task.

Think of this task as solving a puzzle, but not a picture puzzle with only one picture and therefore only one right way to assemble the elements. Instead think of this as a building block type of puzzle with many ways to put the blocks together (to build a house, for example). The key is to have some vision for what you are building. Is it a house, or is it more like a garage, a fort, a tower, or something else? With ideas instead of blocks, the task is more abstract but the principle still applies: Envision your goal.

Follow your vision as a suggestive plan more than as a prescriptive blueprint. Allow for flexibility in the assembly. Try new configurations. Frequently ask *What if?* questions and see what happens when you follow alternatives.

It is usually good to begin with the fixed constraints and the strongest elements. The **fixed constraints** are things that cannot be changed. They are the givens. But before you assume something is a fixed constraint, challenge it. Perhaps people only think it is fixed out of habit; maybe it can be altered. The strongest elements are those elements that receive the highest evaluations. You don't want to ignore these, so begin with them and give them a central place in the synthesis.

Work with the fixed constraints and the strongest elements to determine if they are compatible. If they seem incompatible (i.e., they just do not fit together), then think about what would be needed to help arrange such a fit. To use a very concrete example, perhaps you have a plug that won't fit into your wall outlet. Can you get an adapter that will let you continue with the existing plug and wall outlet and make them both work as is? Or perhaps your fixed constraints and best elements are like oil and water—they just won't mix together. Perhaps you can find a chemical catalyst that you could add to the two and allow them to congeal. To move back to a more abstract level, let's say you are trying to synthesize a process that will solve a problem. You put your fixed constraints in the first step and follow that with your strongest elements, but you know that they will not work together well in that order. In this case, take a larger perspective. Is there something you could build as a middle step in the process between the fixed constraints and the strongest elements? This would be the intervening approach. Or perhaps you could think of something that you could build in as a preparation to the process that would allow the other elements to work better together. This would be an antecedent approach. Or perhaps you could think of a dual-track process where the two sets of incompatible elements would be kept on separate tracks; then perhaps the dual processes each produce their own product, and the products may be compatible.

The synthesis is completed when it attains your goal. That goal is usually utility. At times, you will achieve that goal and still have elements of value left over. In that case, you can ask whether utility would be increased with their addition; if so, you may want to modify your synthesis. If not, then ignore those elements even though they were found to have good value in the evaluation phase of your preparation.

There are times when you might run out of all your elements before you feel the synthesis is complete. That is, perhaps you have been able to incorporate all the elements of value from your evaluation process and yet your synthesis is still missing something—it has gaps in a process or reasoning, or it lacks coherence. In this case, you need to find new messages and re-cycle through the planning process so that you have more elements of value to add to your synthesis. Be careful when you are "adding" these new elements so that they are not simply patched in; instead, they need to be integrated. In order for the product of your synthesis to achieve full utility, each element needs to be added into the construction to fulfill some overall purpose. Think of the process as a journey from your initial condition to the final solution. Each time you add an element, your position along that journey changes, so the route to your destination may change. The shortest distance between your beginning and end points may not be a straight line—there may be barriers in the way.

III. Heuristics

Heuristic 1: Work With Fixed Constraints First

The last step of the algorithm presented above does not provide much detail, so you may be confused about how to assemble elements. It may seem too amorphous of a task and you may be asking, "How can I get started on something like this?" The best way to get started is to begin with the fixed constraints. The fixed constraints are things that cannot be changed. They are the givens.

For example, if you are dealing with a problem about how to spend your money for Christmas presents, the amount of money you have to spend is a fixed constraint. If you have $1,000 to spend, you have many more options to consider than if you have only $40 to spend. If you only have $40, do not spend your time in trial-and-error thinking of combinations of expensive items. This thinking is outside the constraint you are given and therefore this thinking is a waste of time. Another constraint in this problem is the number of people you must buy for. If you must buy presents for four people, then you know each gift should be about $10; that narrows down your options and provides you with a more clear decision path. Another constraint might be that one person is much more important than the other three, so that special person's gift should be about $20 and the other $20 should be divided among the remaining three people.

Working with the constraints first gives more structure to your task. You still need to decide what to buy for each person, but at least you know how much you can spend on each and that brings greater clarity to solving the problem. However, before you assume something is a fixed constraint, challenge it. Perhaps something you thought was a fixed constraint really is not; maybe it can be altered.

Heuristic 2: Too Many Elements

The synthesis is completed when it attains your goal. That goal is usually utility—what you have synthesized is useful as a solution to a problem. At times, you will achieve that goal and still have elements of value left over. In that case, you can ask whether utility would be increased with their addition; if so, you may want to modify your synthesis. If not, then ignore those elements even though they were found to have good value in the evaluation phase of your preparation.

Heuristic 3: Too Few Elements

There are times when you might run out of all your elements before you feel the synthesis is complete. As described above, perhaps you have been able to incorporate all the elements of value from your evaluation process and yet your synthesis is still missing something—it has gaps in a process or reasoning, or it lacks coherence. In this case, you need to find new elements and then re-cycle through the planning process so that you have more elements of value to add to your synthesis. Be careful when you are "adding" these new elements that they are not simply patches that only cover up serious gaps. Instead, they need to be integrated well into a coherent system. If they are not well integrated, then the elements are merely patches that at best only hold a conglomeration of random elements together temporarily, and eventually your synthesized solution to a problem will fall apart.

In order for the product of your synthesis to achieve full utility, each element needs to be added into the construction to fulfill some overall purpose. Think of the process as a journey from your initial condition to the final solution. Each time you add an element, your position along that journey changes and so the route to your destination may change. The shortest distance between your beginning and end points may not be a straight line—there may be barriers in the way.

Heuristic 4: Balance Systematic and Creative Thinking

Performing a synthesis well requires the use of both sides of a person's brain. The left side is needed for systematic reasoning and the right side is needed for creativity. Both sides are needed in balance. If you use the left side of your brain too much, the resulting synthesis will look too much like your old opinion or knowledge structure; there will not be enough elements added to transform it into something fresh. If you use the right side of your brain too much, the resulting synthesis will be too fuzzy to be of good value to you; there will not be enough organization to make all the pieces fit together so there will be inconsistencies and gaps.

IV. Avoiding Traps

There are many traps with synthesis. I will present three of the more general ones in this section. When you get stuck in a synthesis task, think about these traps; it is likely you have fallen into one of them. The more you know about these traps, the better able you will be to get out of them.

Trap 1: Too Complex

Perhaps the most prevalent trap is trying to put too many elements into a synthesis. If you have many elements in your evaluation process and all have been found to have some value, it is tempting to try to fit them all into the synthesis. This is often a mistake. Think about your purpose for the synthesis and let that guide you in deciding how many elements to incorporate into your synthesis. When you have synthesized something (such as a good solution to a problem) that achieves your purpose, end the synthesis process even if you still have elements left over.

There are times, of course, when a synthesis improves with the addition of new elements, but there usually comes a point when the adding of more elements only adds to the complexity rather than the value. Past that point, the synthesis either gets worse or its value stays the same although it becomes more complicated with the forcing in of many additional elements that really don't help the synthesis. Remember that the synthesis is complete when it achieves your purpose.

Trap 2: Expectation of Convergence

Another trap is the expectation of convergence; that is, that there is one best solution. Often, the quest for utility in a synthesis allows for divergence—that is, utility does not require a convergence of thinking so that everyone arrives at only one possible synthesis. Four people working from the same messages and working on the same synthesis task may come up with four different syntheses, each of which has utility. What do you do in this situation? If you must pick only one, then you need to do an evaluation, this time using the syntheses as the messages. The result of this will be an assessment of the relative value of each on some criterion such as utility. What if they are all the same value? Then you will need to bring some outside elements into the consideration process. For example, if the syntheses are proposed solutions for a problem and they all are evaluated as being equal in their potential effect, then an external factor such as cost could be brought in. If each synthesis is equal in terms of what it delivers, then the decision about which to select can be based on which has the lowest resource requirements.

But there is another way to solve the problem of what to do with multiple syntheses. You could conclude that they are all good. Because the process of synthesis requires creativity and this might lead to very different syntheses, we may not be able to put them all on the same continuum for relative comparison. Maybe each is such a different synthesis that each would be rendered as an invidious comparison with another synthesis that is evaluated on a dimension most appropriate for it. In this case, it is best not to force an invidious comparison but instead simply appreciate each for what it is. This is typically the case in seminars with highly intelligent, motivated, and creative students. As the students work off of the same messages, they tend to analyze those messages on different dimensions from one another; they construct compare/contrast categories differently, use different criteria for evaluations, and thus end up with different materials to begin their syntheses and different views for what utility means in the synthesis. In this case, it is better to appreciate the scholarly and creative efforts that brought about each of the different syntheses rather than trying to force a comparison across the syntheses.

Trap 3: Avoiding Completion

Another trap in the process of synthesis is fear of completion. This fear is generated by a nagging feeling that perhaps the solution you synthesized to a problem is not the absolute best one. Often there may be more than one solution to a problem, with each of the various solutions being equally good at solving the problem. If you have synthesized a workable solution that solves the problem, then believe that the synthesis is done and successful. There is no need to test other synthesized solutions to determine which one is best. If your purpose in using synthesis is simply to solve a problem, then it is sufficient to stop when you have synthesized such a solution.

If the required solution to a particular problem has external constraints, then there is a reason to continue with the synthesis if your solution works to solve the problem but does so ignoring those constraints. For example, let's say there are four people working on syntheses to solve a particular problem but the problem has an external constraint of money. That is, a funding agency wants a workable solution to a problem but does not have unlimited funds to enact a solution. In this case, the four people may each devise a workable solution to the problem, but the one requiring the least amount of financial support is the best one because it meets the external constraint the best.

There may be instances when it is not possible to make an adequate comparison and relative evaluation among the different products of synthesis, because they are all products of different types of creative processes. For example, let's say four people are charged with analyzing patriotic messages and arriving at a synthesis of what patriotism means to Americans. One person synthesizes message elements into a poem. Someone else writes a song. The third person makes a wall mural. The fourth person organizes a rally. All can be high-quality syntheses that incorporate a complex of message elements into a larger message that really illustrates the idea of American patriotism. There is no way to develop an adequate single standard to make a fair comparison across all four and chose which one is best. In this situation, it is best to celebrate the diversity of quality.

V. Chapter Review

- The skill of synthesis is more involved than the other skills presented in this book because it involves more steps and the use of other skills, especially analysis, evaluation, and grouping. Its process focuses on analyzing something to identify elements, then evaluating those elements to select those that have the greatest utility to the task at hand. The selected elements are then assembled into a coherent whole.

- Synthesis is used to address two types of challenges. One type is altering something, like a knowledge structure, a belief, or an opinion. This alteration challenge is oriented toward fixing an existing set of ideas and information. The other type is creating something novel, like a new message or a solution to a problem.

- Synthesis is the assembling of elements in a fresh, creative manner. The elements are parts of messages that are identified through analysis and subjected to judgment through evaluation. The synthesis can take the form of a new knowledge structure or the transformation of an older knowledge structure. It can also take the form of a new opinion, a new perspective on a situation, or a solution to a problem.

- The process of synthesizing follows a four-step algorithm of determining purpose, gathering information, selecting the best elements, and assembling those elements. This chapter also provided four heuristics to guide you in working with fixed constraints first, dealing with too many elements, dealing with too few elements, and balancing systematic and creative thinking. It concluded with a caution to avoid the traps of getting caught in too complex a synthesis and expecting convergence.

Exercise 8.1 Practice Using the Synthesis Algorithm

This is a sequence of three challenges designed to increase your understanding of using your skill of synthesizing. This sequence starts with the easiest challenges by providing you with the maximum degree of guidance. As you progress through this sequence, you will find the exercises increasingly challenging because you will have to do more of the thinking for yourself.

Challenge I

1. *Determine Your Purpose:* Think about your favorite video series on broadcast TV, cable TV, or VOD (video on demand). Now that you have watched several episodes of this video series, you are familiar with the characters, settings, and plot structures. You think that you could write a good episode for this video series, so you want to engage in a synthesis.

2. *Gather Information:* Analyze the elements in the video series and answer the following:

   - Who are the main characters?
   - Who are the continuing characters who appear in most episodes although they are not a main character?
   - How many settings typically appear in an episode? What are they?
   - What are the typical plot points?
   - What problems do the characters typically encounter?
   - How do those characters typically go about dealing with those problems?
   - How are those problems typically resolved?

3. *Filter for Acceptable Elements:* Evaluate the elements you have identified in your analysis. Use a personal standard and answer the following:

   - For you, what makes a good character? Keep those characters you like; ignore the rest of the characters.
   - For you, what makes a good setting? Keep the settings you like; ignore the rest.
   - For you, what makes a good plot? Keep the plot points you like the best.

4. *Assemble the Selected Elements Into a Whole:* Group the filtered-in elements (characters, settings, and plots). Use your groupings to create an outline for your episode. You don't need to write the actual script but you do need to decide the following:

   - What problems will be presented to motivate the plot?
   - Which characters are involved in dealing with each problem?

(Continued)

(Continued)

- What will those characters do when they struggle with the problem?
- What setting will be used for each scene?
- How will the problem(s) be resolved by the end of the episode?

After you have assembled all the filtered-in elements (characters, settings, and plots), you might find that they are not enough to complete your outline for the episode. In this case, you will need to think up new characters, settings, and plot points in order to fill in the gaps.

Challenge II

1. *Determine Your Purpose:* There is a particular political issue in your city that greatly interests you. You know that there is a range of opinions on this issue so rather than accept any one of the existing opinions, you decide to use the skill of synthesis to construct your own opinion.

2. *Gather Information:* You get on the Internet and find there are a dozen blogs where citizens argue about this issue.

   - Analyze the material presented in each blog.
   - What will your analytical dimensions be?

3. *Filter for Acceptable Elements:* While there are elements you like in each of these blogs, you feel many of them are presenting faulty arguments.

   - Evaluate the elements you have identified in your analysis.
   - What standards will you use in this evaluation? (Suggestions for standards are things like out-of-date information, inaccurate facts, nonlogical arguments, etc.)
   - Filter out elements that fall short of meeting your standards.

4. *Assemble the Selected Elements Into a Whole:* Take the filtered-in elements from the previous step while ignoring the filtered-out elements. Then group the filtered-in elements.

   - On what characteristics of the elements will you focus in creating your groups?
   - How will you assemble the groupings to create a coherent whole that will easily show potential followers the value of your blog (that is, how your blog is better than any of the alternatives)?

After you have assembled all the filtered-in elements, you might find that they are not enough to construct a coherent and consistent opinion. In this case, you will need to gather additional information to fill in gaps and to resolve discrepancies.

Challenge III

1. *Determine Your Purpose:* Design your ideal career.

2. *Gather Information:* Make a list of possible careers you would like, then gather as much information on each as you can from media sources as well as interviewing people who are in those careers.

   - Analyze the information you have gathered.
   - What will your analytical dimensions be?

3. *Filter for Acceptable Elements:* Evaluate the elements you have identified in your analysis.

   - What standards will you use in this evaluation?
   - Filter in elements that meet your standards, and ignore the rest of the elements.

4. *Assemble the Selected Elements Into a Whole:* Group the filtered-in elements about careers.

   - On what characteristics of the elements about careers will you focus your groups?
   - After you have constructed your groups, think about how distinctive those groups are from one another.

   If the different groups are distinctive from one another, think about how you created such diverse groupings. Does this mean that there are several very different kinds of careers that appeal to you?

   If the different groups are not distinctive from one another, think about collapsing the elements from those different groups into one super-group that describes your vision of an ideal career for you.

   Look at the ideal grouping of characteristics for a career that you have synthesized. Does that description include all the characteristics that you find most valuable or are there some characteristics missing? If some are missing, try incorporating them into your synthesized vision without creating any inconsistencies across elements.

Abstracting

Communicating the Essence of Media Messages

Abstracting is the skill of reducing a **focal object** down into a shorter version that preserves its essence. With media literacy, the focal object is a media message. Abstracting a media message requires people to first understand the essence of the message, then to filter out what is peripheral and to communicate what is core.

Abstracting is not merely listing some of the elements or even all of the elements of a focal object. Nor is it the rank ordering of elements according to the importance of each element. Instead, abstracting is the distilling of the essence of a focal object into a brief description, then communicating that essence in such a way that the full import of the focal object is communicated but in a much shorter space of time.

I. The Abstracting Algorithm

The skill of abstracting relies on some of the other skills of media literacy. Abstracting requires a person first to analyze a focal object to identify its elements, to evaluate those elements on the standard of importance, then to articulate those elements in a way that conveys the central essence of the focal object in brief form (Table 9.1).

Step 1: Determine the Length

The first step in applying the skill of abstracting is to determine how long your abstract is to be. Length is usually specified in number of words for print messages and number of seconds and/or minutes for audio and visual media.

Typically this length limit is given to you. If this is an assignment for a class, your professor will give you this guideline, which is known as a **word budget**. For example, if you are abstracting a short story for a written class assignment, your word budget might be 250 words, which is about one typewritten page (given 12-point Courier with standard 1.5-inch margins). If you are assigned to deliver your abstract orally to a class, then 250 words should take you about 1 minute to deliver.

Do you remember the forms you filled out when you were applying to college? Those forms asked you to write an essay about something in your life and they gave you a word (or page) limit. Those were exercises in abstracting, although they likely never used the term. That is, you were being asked to abstract something from your life, such as a significant event you experienced or something you have been thinking about for a long time (e.g., your goals).

Sometimes you will not be given a length limit before starting the abstract. For example, your friends might be planning to see a movie and know you have already seen the movie, so they ask you what the movie is about.

TABLE 9.1   The Processes of Abstracting

Purpose: To construct a brief, clear accurate description of a message

Pre-task: Conduct an analysis to identify message elements.

Algorithm:

1. Determine how long your abstract is to be.

2. Analyze the focal object.
   a. A component analysis will show you how many topics are in the focal object so that you know how many topics to feature in your abstract.
   b. An outline analysis will go beyond revealing the main components and will also show the structure of ideas within each component.

3. Write an umbrella sentence that conveys the perimeter of the message.

4. If you still have words to use, apportion those words in an equitable manner across all the main elements in the message so that you further develop the main idea in your first sentence in a manner that is balanced across all the main components.

5. Review your abstract to make sure it is complete, balanced, and coherent.

In cases like this, it is good to keep it as short as possible. They don't want a long dissertation with loads of detail. Instead, they typically want a few sentences. If your abstract goes on too long, your friends will get bored and you'll be embarrassed. But if your abstract is too short, your friends will likely ask you questions. It is easier to expand from a good abstract than it is to reduce an abstract that is too long.

Step 2: Analyze the Focal Object

The next step in applying the skill of abstracting is to conduct an analysis of a focal object. A breadth-type approach to analysis would be most useful because you want to make sure that you identify all the important elements in the focal object. Typically you will not have a word budget long enough to go into much, if any, detail while mentioning any of those important elements in your abstract (see Chapter 3).

Step 3: Write an Umbrella Sentence

The third step is to write a sentence that conveys the perimeter of the focal object. Think of this sentence as an umbrella that will cover the essence across the entire span of the focal object. Of course, this will be a very general statement that cannot present much detail. The purpose of this **umbrella sentence** is to alert the reader to what the focal object is while suggesting what the focal object is not.

Step 4: Apportion Additional Words in an Equitable Manner

Most often, the umbrella sentence will not be enough to complete the abstract; that is, you have more words or time to use. In this case, you want to choose your words carefully so that you develop each of the main ideas laid out in the umbrella sentence. For example, your umbrella sentence could be something like "This book was about the ideas of X, Y, and Z." Let's say you have 75 more words to use before reaching your limit. In this case, you would use 25 words to develop each of the ideas X, Y, and Z. Thus you are sharing your word budget equally across each of the three ideas. This is the **balanced strategy**.

The balanced strategy of apportioning words works well if you regard all three ideas to be equally important. However, oftentimes one idea may be more important than the others. In this case, sharing the word budget equally serves to diminish the importance of the most important idea and elevate the importance of the other ideas a bit. Thus, you would send an inaccurate message to your audience and this works against the purpose of abstracting, which is to convey the essence of the focal object as clearly as possible. If you think three ideas are essential to a message but the first of the three is more important, then you should reapportion your 75 words to reflect this (perhaps the major idea should get 35 words, while the other two essential ideas should get 20 words each).

Step 5: Review Your Abstract

When you have assembled all the components (umbrella sentence and sets of sentences for each component), review the assemblage for coverage, balance, and coherence. The **coverage criterion** refers to the completeness of your abstract. Does your first sentence demonstrate enough scope to cover the entire focal object?

The **balance criterion** refers to how you have apportioned your words and time to indicate the relative importance among ideas in the way they communicate the essence of the focal object. If you use most of your words to communicate one particular idea, then your audience will receive the meaning that this idea is the most important one, which is good if that is your intention. So it is important to review your abstract to ensure that you are calibrating the number of words to reflect your belief about the relative importance of ideas in describing the essence of the focal object.

The **coherence criterion** refers to the flow of expression. Have you presented your descriptions in an order that maximizes the communication of what is most important? Will that order be easy for your audience to follow?

II. Heuristics

The challenge of abstracting is a dual one. First, you have to comprehend the message in sufficient depth in order to understand its essence—that is, its essential parts and their relative importance to the overall message. Second, you need to convey those ideas to someone else. You may be able to do the first task well and envision the message very clearly. But often the second task is more challenging. This is frequently the case when your understanding of the message takes the form of an image or feeling; translating images and feelings into words can be very difficult. While some images and feelings may require only a few words to communicate clearly, others seem to require thousands of words. This is a common challenge. I'll present two heuristics below to help deal with these types of challenges.

Heuristic 1: Comprehending the Message

If you do not comprehend the focal object well, you cannot abstract it well. To get started with an abstract, you have to understand what the focal object really is. This requires that we do a good analysis on the focal object, and the analysis typically needs to be more than a cognitive one. For example, if the object is a heart-to-heart conversation with a close friend, the analysis needs emotional and perhaps moral elements, because much of the essence of the conversation is not cognitive. If we overlook the other elements in the message, we will fail to comprehend its essence. If the focal object is a work of art such as a poem, film, or novel, then aesthetic, emotional, and moral elements are likely to be essential for you to adequately understand the message.

Again, this is why our knowledge structures are so important. For example, if we do not have much of an aesthetic knowledge structure with film, then our analysis of the film will lack aesthetic insights or will be composed of faulty aesthetic insights. When these are missing in our understanding, they will certainly also be missing in our abstract.

Heuristic 2: Differential Challenges in Expression

Oftentimes, you will follow all the steps in the abstracting algorithm and carefully arrive at an equitable word budget to showcase the relative importance of each component idea in the focal object. But then you will not be able to stay within the word budget when trying to communicate one particular idea in the abstract. Your dilemma is to either (a) do a poor job communicating about one of your essential ideas because you don't have enough words in your budget for that idea or (b) take some words away from other places in your word budget so you have enough words to do a good job communicating about one of your essential ideas. What do you do? If you choose option (a), your abstract may be faulty because it will fail to communicate an idea you feel is essential and it may even confuse readers. But if you do option (b), then one idea consumes many more words from your word budget and runs the risk of indicating to readers that it is far more important than other ideas that consume many fewer words. This is indeed a dilemma; both options carry risks. When you are confronted with such a problem, remember that the overriding purpose of constructing an abstract is to convey the essence of the focal object to the reader. Thus option (b) is usually better.

Our ability to share information is directly linked to our ability to put emotions and images into words. It takes a good deal of skill to be able to do this at all. And it takes a great deal of skill to be able to do this when your word budget is very small. Fortunately, many of us have close friends who can help us do this. When we have a tough problem that we continue to worry about and we talk to a special friend who really understands us, we only need to use a few words to get across complicated ideas and feelings. Also, a friend may help us clarify things that we are struggling to understand. Somewhere in such a conversation, that special friend may say something to us in a sentence or two that will capture our entire problem; that is, he or she has captured the entire essence of what is bothering us and has been able to express it in a powerfully succinct way. However, many times we are faced with an abstracting challenge where friends cannot help. We have to create understanding on our own.

III. Avoiding Traps

Some of us are able to abstract better than other people. For example, let's say you ask your friend to tell you what happened on the last episode of your favorite medical drama. Your friend says, "A bunch of doctors helped some sick people." Your friend has captured the essence of the show but has not communicated anything unique about that particular episode. Suppose instead that your friend says, "This mugging victim covered with blood was brought in by an ambulance and the medical team went to work checking his vital signs, then a doctor put a tube down his throat so he could breathe." This provides a lot more detail, but it covers only what happened during the few minutes of the hour-long medical drama. A good abstract is one that is detailed enough to convey the essence of the important events in the show but also broad enough so that all the essential happenings are covered. This illustrates the two main traps of abstracting. One of these traps is to reduce the message down so much that the abstract loses its ability to convey the essence of the message. The second trap is to focus on only one part of the message and not convey the full essence.

Trap 1: Overreduction

Let's say the focal object is a novel of 150,000 words or about 350 printed pages. Think of these 150,000 words as forming the base of a pyramid. As we move up the pyramid we reduce the number of words as the sides of the pyramid narrow until we arrive at the point at the very top of the pyramid, which is represented by one word. How far up the pyramid do we need to move to produce a useful abstract? That depends on the purpose of our abstracting. If we move up to about the 100,000-word level, we are in the region of what *Reader's Digest* does with novels when it produces its condensed books. The editors of these condensed novels try to cut out words, paragraphs, and even scenes when they think those elements can be eliminated so that the reader can still follow the plot and understand the characters. If we move further up the pyramid to say the 50,000-word area, we are in the region of the CliffsNotes series. These short paperbacks attempt to capture what happens in each chapter and each scene in as few words as possible. At this level, the abstract is no longer a novel where we see the action unfold and hear the dialogue. Instead, the editor is telling us what happens rather than showing us. As we move up the pyramid more to around the 1,500-word range, we are in the high school term paper area. Here the high school teacher asks us to read the novel then write a paper of about four to six pages in which we describe what happened, the characters, and perhaps the theme. Moving up to about the 150-word level, we are in the encyclopedia range. And near the top of the pyramid at around one to five words is the title. While the titles of most books present their essences, this is usually too small a number of words to be of much use as an abstract.

Any focal object can be abstracted at many different levels, in terms of words or time. However, there is a point of reduction beyond which even the most skilled abstracter cannot convey enough elements to give the reader an adequate idea of the message being abstracted. This varies by the size and complexity of the focal object being abstracted.

Trap 2: Partial Capture

The trap of partial capture is when a person feels she cannot capture the full essence of the focal object in the given word allotment, so she focuses on capturing well only a small part of the message. This approach will end up being unsatisfying to the audience because it is either confusing or it raises questions that it does not answer. Short clips of movie previews are abstracts that exhibit the characteristic of partial capture. The people who create these clips engage in abstracting, but their purpose is to leave the audience with questions as a way of motivating them to buy a ticket to the movie. Thus the purpose of movie previews is less to abstract the movie well and more to stimulate curiosity as a marketing strategy. But abstracts are typically not marketing tools; instead they are instructional vehicles, so they need to inform people about the essence of the focal object rather than tease them.

To avoid this trap of partial capture, it is almost essential to conduct a component analysis first. With this as a first step, you have generated a picture of all the important components that must be captured in the abstract in order for it to be complete. This will also guide you in creating a word budget that will keep you on track by reminding you of the number of topics you must cover, while at the same time limiting you to a set number of words per topic.

IV. Chapter Review

- A good example of abstracting is news coverage. News organizations continually analyze the events each day and evaluate each of those events on importance. Then they select what they deem the most important of those events and put together a package (set of webpages, newspaper, evening news program, etc.) that is an abstract of the day's events.

- Each story in that package is itself an abstract. Each story tells you the central essence of an event. Good news stories typically begin with umbrella sentences that are called lead sentences, which contain the essential information of the who, what, when, where, why, and how. News stories are written to word budgets. Look at how good journalists build off the ideas in the first sentence to expand the treatment of the story.

- When you are looking at news stories, for examples of abstraction, be careful to notice that not all news stories are written as abstracts. Some are written primarily to be attention grabbers, so they do not lead with umbrella sentences that appeal to the mind. Instead they lead with something shocking or intriguing to appeal to the emotions. That type of story structure is more successful at attracting busy audiences, but less successful at conveying the essence of the events of the day.

Exercise 9.1 Practice Using the Abstracting Algorithm

This is a sequence of three challenges designed to increase your understanding of using your skill of abstracting. This sequence starts with the easiest challenges by providing you with the maximum degree of guidance. As you progress through this sequence, you will find the exercises increasingly challenging because you will have to do more of the thinking for yourself.

Challenge I

Think about an episode you viewed from your favorite video series. This selected episode should have one strong story and no subplots. Analyze that episode by focusing on the plot points of what happened during that one episode.

1. *Determine the Length:* You are assigned to write an abstract of 250 words.

2. *Analyze the Focal Object:* Analyze your selected episode for the key plot points. There should be a generating circumstance that gets the story started by introducing a conflict that needs to be solved. The plot

progresses with events that deepen that conflict and make it seem more difficult to resolve. Eventually the conflict is resolved in a climax of action.

3. *Write an Umbrella Sentence:* Write one sentence that captures the essence of the story in that episode.

4. *Apportion Additional Words in an Equitable Manner:* Use a balanced approach. Because the episode had only one story line, think about how many important things happened in that one main story (generating circumstance, events that heightened the conflict, and how the conflict was resolved). Divide the number of those plot points into the remaining words in your budget (this is the 250 words minus the number of words in your umbrella sentence). For example, let's say your umbrella sentence was 20 words and you found five main plot points in the story (one generating circumstance, three events that heightened the conflict, and one resolution event). Using a balanced approach to apportioning your word budget, this would mean that you have 46 words to describe each of those five plot points. Draft out your abstract in six sections: the umbrella sentence and five sections of the main plot points.

5. *Review Your Abstract:* Now that you have drafted out an umbrella sentence and sentences for each of the major plot points, review your draft abstract for three things. First, count the total number of words you have used to make sure you are not exceeding your word budget. Second, make sure that your abstract has covered all the important occurrences in the episode you are abstracting. And third, look at your expression carefully to see if you can express ideas with fewer words (be especially critical of adjectives and adverbs).

Challenge II

Think about an episode you viewed from your favorite video series. This selected episode should have one primary story and several significant secondary stories (subplots that are important but not quite as important as the primary).

1. *Determine the Length:* You are assigned to write an abstract of 250 words.

2. *Analyze the Focal Object:* Analyze the selected episode by listing the key plot points in the primary story and in each of the important subplots.

3. *Write an Umbrella Sentence:* Write one sentence that captures the main thing that happened during that episode.

4. *Apportion Additional Words in an Equitable Manner:* Let's say your analysis of this episode revealed one primary story and two subplots and that your umbrella sentence is 20 words. This leaves you 230 words to apportion among the one primary story and the two subplots. The primary story should get the largest word budget (say, 100 words). This would leave you with 65 words for each of the two subplots. Try using these word indicators as guidelines as you write a first draft of your abstract.

(Continued)

(Continued)

5. *Review Your Abstract:* Now that you have drafted an umbrella sentence and sentences for each of the significant stories in the episode, review your draft abstract for three things. First, count the total number of words you have used to make sure you are not exceeding your word budget, either overall or for each component. Second, make sure that your abstract has covered all the important occurrences in the episode you are abstracting. Third, look at your expression carefully to see if you can express ideas with fewer words (be especially critical of adjectives and adverbs).

Challenge III

1. *Determine the Length:* Think about the entire video series—not just one episode—and write a 500-word abstract.

2. *Analyze the Focal Object:* In this exercise, the focal object is the full set of episodes throughout the entire video series. Analyze the series by listing the key plot points in the primary story and in each of the important subplots that span across episodes.

3. *Write an Umbrella Sentence:* Write one sentence that captures the main story that runs through the entire series.

4. *Apportion Additional Words in an Equitable Manner:* Determine your own word budget. Think about the relative importance of various story lines and apportion words that reflect how important each of those story lines is.

5. *Review Your Abstract:* Now that you have drafted an umbrella sentence and sentences for each of the significant stories in the series, review your draft abstract for three things: equitable word budgeting, completeness, and expression.

After you have completed the above sequence of three challenges that guide you in practicing your skill of abstracting, you may want to continue practicing. So go through the sequence again but change the focal object to something else such as a novel, a nonfiction book, a Facebook page, an advertising campaign, or a multiplayer video game that takes place in a virtual world.

Exercise 9.2 Abstracting Media Messages

1. Read 20 news stories in a newspaper.

   - Classify each story as either being an example of an abstract or not.

   - For each story, list the ideas set up in the lead (umbrella) sentence. Then circle and label each of those ideas that are developed in the rest of the story.

- Are all ideas treated equally? If not, why do you think some of those ideas warranted more words than others?

2. Create a cognitive abstract.

   - Read a chapter in one of your textbooks.

   - Write a 200-word abstract that captures the full essence of the ideas in that chapter.

3. Create an emotional abstract.

   - Listen to a news pundit talk emotionally about some controversial issue. Find a website or video channel where people are highly involved in heated debates. Write a 200-word abstract that conveys the emotions that pundit was expressing. You will likely need to include information about the issue itself but present that information as a way to contextualize the emotions. Place the focus of your abstract on conveying the emotions of the pundit more so than on conveying information about the essence of the issue.

   - Write an umbrella sentence that conveys the overriding emotions presented in the news pundit's presentation. What emotion was the pundit exhibiting? What emotions was the pundit trying to trigger in the audience?

4. Create a moral abstract.

   - Listen to a news pundit talk about some controversial issue (it can be the same media message as you used in item 3 immediately above). Write a 200-word abstract that conveys the moral dimension of the issue in that media message. Place the focus of your abstract on conveying the moral implications of the issue more so than on conveying information about the essence of the issue itself.

   - Write an umbrella sentence that conveys the core moral issue in the pundit's presentation. Did the pundit recognize what the moral issue was, and if so, what did she or he recommend to the audience?

5. Create an aesthetic abstract.

   - Pick a movie or television show you recently saw. Write a 200-word abstract about the aesthetic quality of the show. The foreground of the abstract should be your reaction to the aesthetic quality. Telling the reader what happened in the show or who the characters were should be in the background.

   - Write an umbrella sentence to present your strongest aesthetic judgment—that is, what was the best or worst aesthetic element (writing, acting, directing, editing, sound, music, costumes, set designs, special effects, etc.). Budget your remaining words to explain the essence of the quality. For example, if you thought the writing was particularly strong, then you will need to talk about what happened in the plot, but don't present a synopsis of the plot; instead, talk about the plot in a way to show why it was such a high-quality story.

(Continued)

(Continued)

6. Write a multidimensional abstract.

- Think about a novel you have read. Think about what happened and its characters. Think about the emotions it evoked. Think about the moral dilemmas for the characters. Think about the quality of the writing. Which of these thoughts dominates? That is, in which areas do you feel the essence of the book lies? Write a 500-word abstract.

- Write an umbrella sentence that captures the essence of the book (cognitively, emotionally, morally, and aesthetically). With good novels, all these elements are intertwined but one or two will dominate. Then budget your remaining words to address all four categories (cognitive, emotional, moral, and aesthetic). When you write about each of these four, show how they are all related. Also, make sure the ideas you express when writing about each of the four would fall under the umbrella sentence.

Exercise 9.3 Nonmedia Abstracting

1. Create a cognitive abstract.

- Observe some occurrence in your own life. It need not be newsworthy in the journalistic sense but it should involve several people engaged in some action.

- Write a 200-word news-type story that captures the essence of that occurrence. Present information about the who, what, when, where, and why.

2. Create an emotional abstract.

- Pick a person you like and write a 100-word abstract focusing purely on emotions. What are the emotions this person typically exhibits? Write an umbrella sentence to capture the answer to that question. Then budget your remaining words to develop a description about how that person exhibits each of those emotions.

- Pick a person you do not like very much and write a 100-word abstract focusing purely on emotions. What are the emotions this person typically exhibits? Write an umbrella sentence to capture the answer to that question. Then budget your remaining words to develop a description about how that person exhibits each of those emotions.

3. Create a moral abstract (200 words).

   - Pick an ethical issue. It can be a big issue on the national agenda such as prayer in schools, abortion, gun control, school privatization, and so on. Or you might have an ethical issue confronting you in your personal life.

   - Write a 200-word abstract focusing attention on the essence of that issue. Typically ethical issues have at least two sides, so your umbrella sentence should present both sides. Then budget your remaining words to develop the pros and cons of each side.

   - Write an abstract focusing on your personal belief on that issue. Blend the moral and the emotional. Write an umbrella sentence that presents your position. Then budget your remaining words to develop the emotions and reasons to elaborate your position.

4. Create an aesthetic abstract.

   - Pick a nonmedia focal object that can be evaluated aesthetically. For example, you could focus on how beautiful (or ugly) your college campus is, on how well one of your friends dresses, or on a nonmediated work of art (e.g., a painting, sculpture, etc.). Write a 200-word abstract about the aesthetic quality of that focal object. Foreground your reaction to the aesthetic quality of that focal object.

   - Write an umbrella sentence to present your strongest aesthetic judgment; that is, what is the best or worst aesthetic element? Budget your remaining words to explain the essence of the quality.

5. Write a multidimensional abstract (500 words).

   - Think about some recurring behavioral pattern exhibited by one of your friends. Think about how that continual behavior makes you feel. Think about the moral dilemma that may be underlying that behavior. Think about how skilled your friend is with that behavior.

   - Write an umbrella sentence that captures the essence of the nature of your friend's behavior pattern and your reaction to it—what it is, how it makes you feel, what moral issues it raises in you, and how well your friend performs that behavior. Then budget your remaining words to address all four categories (cognitive, emotional, moral, and aesthetic). When you write about each of these four, show how they are all related. Also, make sure the ideas you express when writing about each of the four would fall under the umbrella sentence.

Putting It All Together

Congratulations! You have made it all the way to the last chapter. By this point, you should have a good appreciation of the essential skills you have been using—or not using—every day as you have been encountering media messages throughout your entire life. By doing the exercises at the end of each of the skills chapters, you should have a detailed understanding about the level of ability that you have already developed with each of these seven skills. The journey you have made by reading through the chapters in this book, diagnosing your level of skills, and beginning to develop higher levels on those skills has already been significant. And that journey can continue as you incorporate what you have learned into your processing of media messages from this point forward. What you have already learned will pay off in increases in your ability to use media messages to meet your needs better, and thereby avoid the risks of being exploited by the designers of those media messages who are solely interested in using you as a tool to meet their own needs. The knowledge you have acquired has given you that power, and that power will increase the more you use it.

You now have enough knowledge to continue this journey on your own. By reading through the book up to this point, you know the basic algorithm of each of these seven skills. You know that the algorithms oftentimes are not enough and that you will have to use heuristics. You know what many of the traps are and how to avoid them. Now what you need is the motivation to continue on the journey. So I leave you with a pep talk that I hope will encourage you to continue on this journey of gradually and continually improving your skills and thereby become an ever more powerful thinker and user of the media.

I. Pep Talk

To help you on your continuing journey, I'll leave you with seven ideas. I hope you will use these ideas to guide your mastery of the skills presented in this book.

1. Remember That Your Skills Can Always Be Improved

No matter what level your skills are now, they can always be improved. Skills are like muscles. If you know how to work out well, your muscles will get stronger and stronger. But if you continually neglect them, they will get weaker and weaker. So ask yourself whether you want to get stronger or weaker.

Do not get depressed if one or more of your skills is currently weak. We are born with certain levels of abilities on these skills. Some people seem so lucky to have been born with greater abilities than us. That seems unfair. Aren't we all supposed to have been created equal? That is a nice saying but it has never been true. What is true is that we are rarely stuck permanently with the natural abilities with which we were born—we can improve! But improvement requires two things. First, improvement requires guidance. This manual has given you a great deal of specific guidance. Second, improvement requires work. You need to use the guidance to exercise your skills. The more you exercise in the right way, the more your skills become powerful.

You have attained your current level of media literacy skills through a combination of factors that include maturation, conditioning, and work. Your beginning place was determined by some genetic factors, but by now you are well beyond the point where maturation can be depended upon for further development. Since elementary school, your progress in developing these skills has been shaped largely through reward and punishment. If you have been getting good feedback to help you improve and have experienced frequent feelings of reward, then your skills have likely developed well. In contrast, if you have felt overwhelmed in trying to use these skills and have frequently felt punished when you have used them, then you have likely avoided using these skills and therefore they have not improved much if at all.

You are not stuck with your current skill levels for life. Skill levels are constantly changing. The good news is that you can do things to strengthen your skills. The bad news is that if you do not work at maintaining your existing skills, they will grow weaker. So the key question is: Do I want to upgrade my skills or let them degrade?

There is a saying that practice makes perfect. With skill development, this does not hold because we can never get to a place of perfection—a goal of perfection is unrealistic. But practice does make us better. And the more practice, the better.

2. The Seven Skills Work Together, So Develop Them All

As you have seen in reading this manual, these skills often work together in combination. For example, the skill of analysis is typically needed to identify elements in media messages in order to use any of the other skills because the other six skills need those elements as raw materials in their usage. Also, as you have seen, the grouping skill works closely with the skills of induction and deduction. With induction, you look for patterns across elements. In essence, this is the task of comparing—that is, determining what the elements have in common. When you find a pattern, you infer the rule that allows you to group all those elements together. With deduction, the rule is the major premise and your observation of an element is the minor premise. If the element meets the rule, it in essence is classified as being an example of the rule and the rule applies; thus you are comparing the element to the rule. If the element does not meet the rule, it is classified as not being an example of the rule; thus you are contrasting the element with the rule. In order to use your grouping skill well, you also have to be skilled at induction and deduction. Because of the way skills work together in various combinations, it is important to develop all of your skills in a balanced manner so that you acquire strength in using them in any combination.

Again, think of skills as muscles. If you put all of your exercise effort into developing only your upper body strength, you are likely to end up with strong shoulders, pecs, and biceps but your lower body then might be too weak to carry around such a huge upper body. Powerful athletes know that the body's muscles are all part of a system and that the development of any one muscle group needs to be balanced by the development of the other muscle groups so that they can all work together well at each higher level of strength. The strongest people are those whose total set of muscles are strong in a complete and balanced manner. With media literacy, the most successful people are those who have high levels of development across all seven of these skills. If you continue to develop all seven of these skills, you will grow stronger in exerting control over your media exposures, extracting the meanings that benefit you most, and using those exposures to grow the pleasure in your life while avoiding risks of letting negative influences manipulate you.

3. Value Creativity and Intuition

While it is important to start with rules and algorithms to give structure to your exercises, oftentimes these will only get you so far. To complete many tasks, especially when working with partially specified problems, you also need creativity to work with heuristics. Both systematic thinking and creative thinking are essential for the continued development of your media literacy skills.

As for systematic thinking, understand the algorithms. These algorithms are rules that have been developed over millennia of human thinking and problem solving. The better you can apply these algorithms, the more structure and clarity will you have to your thinking. Creative thinking is also important. Creative thinking helps you "jump the gaps" that you will continually find in the process laid out by the algorithms. The rules can get you started, but you also need heuristics to stimulate your thinking so you can work around barriers that will inevitably present themselves.

4. Skills Are More Important than Information or Facts

In our information-rich culture, getting access to any type of fact is no longer a problem. Our workforce is now dominated by information workers. The percentage of the American workforce employed in information generating and processing jobs jumped from 17% of the total workforce in 1950 to more than 65% by 1980 (Naisbitt, 1982) and the percentage is still growing. Half of all the scientists who have ever lived are alive today and producing information. Also, there are more engineers, doctors, writers, historians, psychologists, and others producing more information than ever before. And they are all producing information that is easily available on the Internet.

This information, however, becomes outdated quickly. So the value we get from memorizing facts today will start to dwindle tomorrow until within a few years that value has eroded away. In contrast, the value of our skills increases with time if we continue to use and improve them. Now the primary challenge for people in our culture is to do something of value with information they experience every day. How well you are continually able to meet this challenge is keyed to how well you have developed your seven skills of media literacy.

5. Be Skeptical

Don't accept things as they appear on the surface in media messages. Analyze them—dig below the surface to understand what those messages are really saying. Don't rely so much on other people's evaluations, groupings, inductions, deductions, and syntheses. Work things through for yourself. If your skills are strong, you will likely be able to do these things better for yourself because you will be using these skills as tools to serve your own goals; therefore, the products of these efforts will fit much better into your knowledge structures.

Don't be satisfied with your existing knowledge structures. They may contain facts that are out of date or faulty in some way. Also, they may be too limited; you need more. And they may contain beliefs that are faulty, so that when you use these beliefs as standards when you evaluate things, you will end up making judgments that are counterproductive.

The media used to provide a strong filtering function. That is, traditional news organizations had editors with significant professional experience to check facts so that what was presented as news could be trusted as being accurate. Now that interactive platforms are so common, most of the information we encounter through media exposures is unfiltered. You cannot assume that what is presented as a fact has any value to you. Now the default perspective on media information should be skepticism rather than trust.

6. Pay More Attention to Your Personal Goals

Skills are tools that you use to achieve goals. Therefore, the building of stronger skills should take place inside a goal-directed perspective. We need to have some goals for our lives and how media exposures fit into what we want our lives to be. Skills then become valuable as a means for achieving those goals. The expectation of reaching our goals sustains us when we find parts of the process very challenging.

We must be careful that we don't spend all our time developing skills just for the sake of developing skills. If we do this, we will undoubtedly fall into one of two traps. One is what I call the "Medieval Scholar" trap, where you work on skills solely for the sake of building your skills and showing off. Thus you get into a lot of discussions about how many angels can dance on the head of a pin. Such discussions can be interesting as mental calisthenics from time to time, but when they become a way of life, you are trapped inside nonproductive activities. We need to be careful we do not exercise our mental muscles to the point of becoming muscle bound; that is, we spend all our time developing muscles just for the sake of having muscles and eventually find ourselves unable to use them to do any useful work other than to "work out" and develop more muscles.

Another trap is what I call "I'm not good enough yet." People who are stuck in this trap work very hard on their skills but never feel they get to a point of competence, so they never get value out of all their effort. Don't be like a person who goes to the hardware store every day shopping for new tools in order to stock his workshop but then never actually uses the tools to make anything. Skills are tools. They have little value unto themselves; they become valuable when they are used to build or fix something worthwhile.

Some of your goals may not be as specific as others (such as earning at least a 3.6 GPA and gaining admission to graduate school). More than likely, your most important goals will be something like these:

- To lead an interesting and productive life.

- To find challenges of all kinds and excel at meeting them.

- To understand more about the world and my place in it.

When we have broad, general goals, it is important to set objectives, which serve as milestones along the way to achieving our broad goals in life. These milestones keep us focused and provide us with a sense of progress as we pass each one. When you pass a milestone for your current objective, let yourself feel great. But also realize that there needs to be another marker to guide the next part of your journey and on and on until you eventually reach your goal.

7. Commit to the Investment in Your Future

Think of the work in developing your skills of media literacy as an investment. For many of us, it is very difficult to put our money in a savings account rather than spend it on things to make us feel better today. But if we do make sacrifices today and invest some money, that money will grow through compounding over time and come back to us in a much larger amount in the future. And at that time, we will be able to buy more substantial rewards for ourselves that will more than pay us back for all the small sacrifices we make along the way.

Getting started requires an investment of effort from you. In the beginning, it may be difficult to get used to doing the exercises. But when you commit to investing your time and effort to strengthen your skills, you will begin the road toward a much bigger reward. Improvement will be slow at first, but if you keep investing your effort, the improvements will begin coming at a more rapid rate. Once you start noticing the improvements, the work will get easier and more rewarding. With even more work, the improvements will come faster and be more dramatic. The payoff comes in the form of being able to make faster and better decisions when encountering new information, working with that information, and sharing that knowledge.

The earlier you get started in this investment of time and energy, the greater the payoffs will be. But don't expect a linear relationship between the amount of effort you put in and the amount of payoff you get. A linear relationship is the return of one unit of output for each one unit of input. For example, if our rate of pay is $10 per hour and we work 1 hour, we expect to be paid $10—that is, one unit of work (the hour) translates into one unit of pay (hourly rate). If we put two units in, we expect two units out. Linear thinking leads us to believe that for each unit of effort we put into a task, we should get one unit of return; thus, there is a one-to-one correspondence between effort and return. If we work 10 hours and we expect to get paid $100 but instead are paid $80, then that is not fair. We have been cheated out of 2 hours of pay, because we naturally expect a linear relationship between hours and pay.

It is a mistake to expect a linear relationship when it comes to improving your seven skills of media literacy. If you make this mistake, you will greatly overestimate the return you expect immediately and will greatly underestimate the return you will get in the long term. Instead, you should set your expectations by the learning curve (see Figure 10.1). The learning curve shows the relationship between effort and return. With the strengthening of skills, the "effort" is something like hours of study or units of concentration, and the "return" is something like the degree of strength with a skill. The dotted line is straight, thus indicating a linear relationship. But the dotted line illustrates a linear one-to-one relationship, while the solid line illustrates the learning curve. Let's take a closer look at the learning curve line. Notice that as the line moves right (more units of effort), it does not move up (units of output) very much. This indicates that when your skill level is low, it takes a lot of effort to get it to move up much. That is, you keep putting in effort (moving to the right on the effort line) but you don't get much return (elevation off the effort line). However, if you continue putting in effort, you will eventually reach the "break point" where the returns start to move up at an accelerating rate.

Most people quit before they reach the break point. Why? They are trapped by linear thinking. They think that the relationship between the reward they have been receiving for all the effort they are expending so far in the early stages of an exercise plan will continue forever. They think that the ratio of many units of effort required for such a small amount of return will go on and on and on and not change. They conclude that they will always have to work too hard for too little gain, so they quit.

Those people who are not trapped by linear thinking know that if they stick to the task, they will eventually reach the break point, and they will be getting greater returns on their effort. These people know that in the early stages of a task, they are simply "paying their dues" and they don't expect much in return. They have faith that their hard work will eventually pay off. Furthermore, they know that they will eventually reach the point of fairness where they will have received a number of reward units equal to the number of effort units.

If you can stick it out through the dues-paying phase and reach the break point, then everything becomes easier and you start feeling that it is fun. Remember when you were learning to ride a bicycle? The first few days were so frustrating because you would practice and practice but not seem to get it. You saw so little improvement in your riding that you wondered if you would ever be able to ride by yourself without training wheels. Then one day you suddenly "got it." You were riding by yourself and it felt so good, you couldn't stop smiling! Then in the next few days you were learning so many things so quickly. You learned how to go faster and to maneuver around obstacles. And a few days later you were even showing off, riding with no hands and even standing on your seat. You were able to get past the early frustration of high effort with a seemingly total lack of progress. But then once you started experiencing success, it came at a very rapid pace. Eventually you got to the point where maintaining your balance—even through sharp turns—required almost no effort at all.

The most rewarding part of the learning curve is when you move beyond the "break point" to where you get back more than you put in. In this area, you appear to be doing things with little effort and you seem to be much more successful than are other people who are working hard and not being successful. Those struggling people may be looking at you and thinking, "If she/he can do it so easily, why can't I? Am I stupid? What is wrong with me?" What is wrong with them is that there is a kink in their thinking that prevents them from understanding the nonlinear relationship between effort and reward. Many people do not have this important insight, so they do not make it to the break point.

There's one more thing to consider about nonlinear thinking. The learning curve line in Figure 10.1 is a smooth line; that is, there are no bumps along its curve. But if we could plot the actual relationship in any specific situation, the line would not be a smooth curve. It would have lots of little bumps and dips along the way. Think of the road map of the United States, where the interstate highways are shown as relatively straight lines compared to the actual twists and turns they make as they swing around particular hills and follow along the bends of rivers. When you exercise your skills of media

FIGURE 10.1   **The Learning Curve: Expressing the Relationship of Return on Effort**

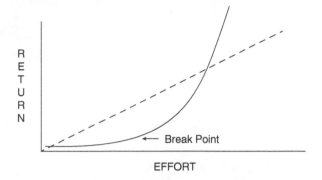

literacy, you will have some days where nothing will go right and other days when things will go better than expected. However, it is important that you keep your thinking on the bigger picture, which is the overall pattern of the upward-moving learning curve.

II. Conclusion

When you continually challenge yourself to develop your skills, you will become a more powerful thinker. When you think more powerfully, you get much more in return for your effort. This is highly rewarding, because you are able to figure things out better than other people; you are able to see more connections among things compared to other people; you are able to create better and more creative solutions to problems than other people; and you are able to tell all of these things to other people in a clear and persuasive manner. All of this is highly rewarding. These rewards are so attractive, you will want to experience them again and again. When you reach this point, learning is no longer work; it becomes pure fun.

Now, go out and see how much fun you can have!

References

Anderson, C. (2006). *The long tail: Why the future of business is selling less of more.* New York, NY: Hyperion.

Angwin, J. (2009). *Stealing MySpace: The battle to control the most popular website in America.* New York, NY: Random House.

Brown, J. A. (1991). *Television "critical viewing skills" education: Major media literacy projects in the United States and selected countries.* Hillsdale, NJ: Lawrence Erlbaum.

Copi, I. M. (1978). *Introduction to logic.* New York, NY: Macmillan.

eMarketer. (2014 April). Time spent per day with major media in the United States from 2009 to 2014 (in minutes). *Statista—The Statistics Portal.* Retrieved January 17, 2015 from https://www.statista.com

eMarketer. (2017, May 1). US adults now spend 12 hours 7 minutes a day consuming media: US adults will spend more than half the day with major media. Retrieved May 26, 2018 from https://www.emarketer.com/Article/US-Adults-Now-Spend-12-Hours-7-Minutes-Day-Consuming-Media/1015775

Goleman, D. (1995). *Emotional intelligence.* New York, NY: Bantam Books.

Haven, K. (2007). *Story proof: The science behind the startling power of story.* Westport, CT: Libraries Unlimited.

Matthews, J. (1992, April 13). To yank or not to yank? *Newsweek,* p. 59.

McCawley. J. D. (1981). *Everything linguists have always wanted to know about logic.* Chicago, IL: University of Chicago Press.

McLaren, P., Hammer, R., Sholle, D., & Reilly, S. (Eds.) (1995). *Rethinking media literacy: A critical pedagogy of representation.* New York, NY: Peter Lang Publishing, Inc.

Messaris, P. (1994). *Visual "literacy": Image, mind, and reality.* Boulder, CO: Westview.

Naisbitt, J. (1982). *Megatrends: Ten new directions transforming our lives.* New York, NY: Warner Books Inc.

National Center for Education Statistics. (2012). Program for International Student Assessment. Retrieved February 5, 2009 from http://nces.ed.gov/surveys/pisa/index.asp

Pingdom. (2019). 2018 – Pingdom year in review. Retrieved January 17, 2019 from https://royal.pingdom.com/2019/01/09/2018-pingdom-year-in-review/

Pinker, S. (1997). *How the mind works.* New York, NY: W. W. Norton & Company.

Potter, W. J. (1987). Does television viewing hinder academic achievement among adolescents? *Human Communication Research, 14*, 27–46.

Quine, W. V. O. (1972). *Methods of logic.* New York, NY: Holt, Rinehart, & Winston.

Schwartz, B. (2016, November 14). Google's search knows about over 130 trillion pages. Retrieved January 5, 2019 from https://searchengineland.com/googles-search-indexes-hits-130-trillion-pages-documents-263378

Silver, N. (2012). *The signal and the noise: Why so many predictions fail—but some don't.* New York, NY: Penguin.

Silverblatt, A. (1995). *Media literacy: Keys to interpreting media messages.* Westport, CT: Praeger.

Storr, W. (2014). *The unpersuadables: Adventures with the enemies of science.* New York, NY: Overlook Press.

Strauss, R. (1996, November 29). The numbers game. *Los Angeles Times*, p. E4.

Thompson, C. (2009, September). The new literacy. *Wired*, p. 48.

Tucker, P. (2014). *The naked future: What happens in a world that anticipates your every move?* New York, NY: Current.

U.S. Census Bureau. (2017). *Statistical abstract of the United States: 2016*. Washington, DC: Department of Commerce.

WorldWideWebSize.com. (2019, January 5). The size of the World Wide Web (the Internet). Retrieved January 5, 2019 from https://www.worldwidewebsize.com/

YouTube. (2018). YouTube in numbers. Retrieved May 22, 2018 from https://www.youtube.com/intl/en-GB/yt/about/press/

Glossary

Abstracting: The assembling of elements into a brief, clear, and accurate description of a message.

Aesthetic standards: Benchmarks people use to judge the artistic quality of a message.

Algorithms: Brescriptions as guides to solving problems that are formulas or lists of steps; they are adequate for solving fully specified problems but not partially specified problems.

Alteration challenge: Using the skill of synthesis to make changes to an existing complex of ideas.

Analysis: Examining an object to identify its elements.

Analytical dimensions: An array of components that can be used to guide any analysis.

Analyzing: The breaking down of a message into meaningful elements.

Automatic routines: Programs that run unconsciously in human brains; some of these routines are common to all humans because they are already part of our brains at birth; some are learned through experience.

Automaticity: A mental state where our minds operate without any conscious effort from us.

Balance criterion: During the process of reviewing drafts of an abstract, this criterion focuses attention on whether the abstract communicates what is most important through the relative number of words used to express each component.

Balanced strategy: Apportioning words or time in an abstract in an equal manner across each major component of the focal object.

Breadth approach: Focuses your attention on using analysis to increase your understanding of the span of elements within the media message.

Category constructing heuristic: Guidelines for deciding how to divide a continuous distribution into categories in a nonarbitrary manner.

Classification reasoning: Using a syllogism with one major premise and one minor premise to determine if the observation in the minor premise belongs in the category as the rule in the major premise states.

Classification scheme: The set of characteristics you use to guide comparing and contrasting when using the skill of grouping.

Cognitive standards: Benchmarks that make something satisfying to the mind, such as accuracy or utility.

Coherence criterion: During the process of reviewing drafts of an abstract, this criterion focuses attention on whether the abstract presents ideas in a clear flow of meaning

Combination approach: Focuses your attention on using analysis to increase your understanding about the full set of elements—both in scope and in depth—presented in a media message.

Competencies: Abilities to perform simple tasks; they are categorical (i.e., either a person can perform the task successfully or not).

Component analysis: Examining a message to identify its major modules along an analytical dimension.

Conceptual differentiation: The natural ability to classify things; people at higher levels of this ability are able to classify things into many categories and subcategories because they see many differences and many similarities across objects to be classified.

Conclusion: The third and final statement in a syllogism; it is derived through a process of logical reasoning using the first two statements in a syllogism – the major premise and the minor premise.

Conditional reasoning heuristic: Guidelines to conduct reasoning when the major premise is conditional; that is, there may be other major premises that are relevant conditions that must be considered in the process of reasoning to a conclusion.

Coverage criterion: During the process of reviewing drafts of an abstract, this criterion focuses attention on whether the abstract is complete enough to convey the full span of essence of the focal object.

Creation challenge: Using the skill of synthesis to assemble something novel.

Criteria of standards: The conditions that must be met to achieve the standard.

Crystalline intelligence: The ability to memorize facts, images, definitions, opinions, and agendas of others.

Deducing: The using of general principles to explain particulars in a process of logical reasoning.

Defining purpose heuristic: A means of clarifying your purpose for the analysis after you have begun the analysis.

Depth approach: Focuses your attention on using analysis to increase your understanding about a particular element among the set of elements presented in a media message.

Element: An individual unit in the object being analyzed.

Emerging classification scheme heuristic: Guidelines for developing a classification scheme while you are doing the classifications themselves.

Emotional intelligence: The natural ability to understand one's own emotions, to control those emotions, and to read emotions in other people.

Emotional standards: Expectations that a message should evoke a particular emotional reaction in a person.

Evaluating: Making judgments about the value of an element; the judgment is made by comparing the element to some standard.

Factual information: Discrete bits of information, such as names (of people, places, characters, events, etc.), definitions of terms, formulas, lists, and the like; a fact is something raw, unprocessed, and context free.

Falsification heuristic: Finding evidence counter to a general claim so that the claim can be altered to make it less general or rejected altogether.

Field dependency: A cognitive ability that focuses on the degree to which people are able to separate signal from noise in any experience; *signal* refers to elements in an experience that help a person interpret the meaning of that experience, while *noise* refers to the chaos of elements peripheral or irrelevant to this task.

Field of elements: The full set of all elements in the object being analyzed.

Fixed constraints: Things in a problem that are givens and cannot be changed; they serve to limit your degrees of freedom in thinking about options to solve the problem.

Fluid intelligence: The ability to be creative, to challenge what we see on the surface, to look deeper and broader, and to recognize new patterns in complex sets of facts.

Focal object: The thing that is abstracted; with media literacy, the focal object is a media message.

Fully specified problem: A cognitive challenge that provides enough information in the way the problem is presented that we can use learned algorithms to arrive at the one and only one correct solution.

General claim: Argument that the pattern found in the elements you observed extends to a larger class of elements you have not observed.

Generalize: Make a claim that a pattern you infer from observing a small number of elements within a set is the same pattern you would find if you examined all the elements in that set.

Grouping: Determining which elements are alike in some way; determining which elements are different in some way.

Heuristics: Suggested guidelines, recommendations, tools, and shortcuts that we use to solve problems, especially partially specified problems.

How many groups? heuristic: Guidelines for determining how many categories to use in your classification scheme.

Identifying number of elements heuristic: A means of determining how many options exist along an analytical dimension after starting the analysis.

Identifying number of levels heuristic: A means of determining how deeply an outline analysis should go.

Inducing: The inferring of general patterns from the observation of particulars; generalizing those patterns to larger aggregates; and the continual testing of those patterns.

Inductively derived positions on dimensions heuristic: A means of identifying analytical dimensions after you have begun your analysis.

Information: Content of messages that can be either factual or social.

Intuition: The direct perception of truths without any reasoning process.

Knowledge structures: Information stored in a person's mind in an organized manner so that it can be easily recalled; they are constructed by the person.

Lateral thinking: In contrast to vertical thinking, this is thinking "outside the box" or getting off the purely logical lock-step path to solving problems; it is more creative and relies on sudden insights to reveal new ways of approaching a solution to difficult problems.

Linear reasoning: Start with two premises and reason to a third, but in this case, we cannot identify one of the premises as being major and one as minor; instead both premises operate at the same level of generality (that is, they are both general principles or they are both observations).

Major premise: The first statement in a syllogism; a general principle or rule.

Maturation: As a factor that determines a person's level of skills, maturation refers to how much a person's brain has developed mainly in childhood.

Mental codes: The programming in our brains that runs automatic routines of thinking and behaving.

Message: A vehicle that delivers information to us; messages can be delivered in many different media (television, radio, CDs, video games, books, newspapers, websites, conversations, lectures, concerts, signs along the streets, labels on the products we buy, etc.); they can be large (an entire Hollywood movie) or small (one utterance by a friend) and complex (a philosopher's metaphysical position laid out in a dense book) or simple (a common word).

Metaphor: A tool that helps in lateral thinking where we get out of the problem itself and think about something that resembles the problem, which can give us a fresh perspective on the problem.

Minor premise: The second statement in a syllogism; usually an observation of a particular thing that is relevant to the general principle stated in the major premise.

Moral standards: Benchmarks that make something satisfying to a person's code of ethics or religion.

Multiple characteristics heuristic: Guidelines for using more than one characteristic simultaneously in categorizing elements.

Multiple elements heuristic: Guidelines for making a summary evaluative judgment when multiple elements are being evaluated at the same time.

Naïve scientists: People using the inductive method in their everyday lives.

Natural abilities: Those skills and competencies that we are born with; they can be cognitive or emotional.

Noncategorical scheme heuristic: Guidelines for transforming characteristics with continuous values into categories; sometimes the characteristics that you use to classify elements are not categorical and instead are a continuum of values.

Nonimpulsiveness: A natural ability to control one's emotions when dealing with information so that one does not become quickly frustrated by tasks but instead is willing to work through ambiguities.

Object: The thing that is being analyzed; it can be tangible (such as a physical object) or intangible (such as an element).

Partially specified problem: A cognitive challenge that does not provide enough information in the way the problem is presented that we can use learned algorithms to arrive at the one and only one correct solution; instead partially specified problems require the use of heuristics to fill in missing information to arrive at a useful solution where there is typically more than one useful solution.

Personal judgment: A tool to use with heuristics in filling in gaps in the problem-solving process.

Personal locus: This is the combination of goals and drives that guides a person in the use and improvement of the skills of media literacy; *goals* refer to a plan that comes from a person's awareness of self and the needs for exposures to media messages, and *drives* refer to a person's cognitive energy that propels the person to increase his or her level of media literacy.

Population: The total set of all possible elements to which you are generalizing; you almost never are able to observe all elements in the population because the number of such elements is too large.

Primitive classification heuristic: Oftentimes we make classifications without the benefit of a complete set of rules; instead we learned to classify through trial and error where we have developed an intuitive sense of what characteristics are most associated with common groupings, like dogs.

Probability premise heuristic: Guidelines to conduct reasoning when the major premise is not absolute and instead is based on a probability.

Sample: The number of elements within a population that you have observed.

Searching: looking for one particular element in a field.

Self improvement: Actions taken by an individual to increase one's level of media literacy by improving one's skill set.

Skills: Cognitive tools that we use to access information in media messages, then transform that information into knowledge structures by recognizing and constructing meaning.

Social information: Beliefs about the social world that are derived through interpretation.

Standard: An essential component of any evaluation; the process of evaluation is the comparing of some element to the standard to determine how well the element meets the standard.

Standard-complex: A standard used in an evaluation where the standard is an amalgamation of multiple criteria.

Synthesis: The skill used to assemble individual elements into a coherent whole.

Synthesizing: The assembling of elements into a novel structure to solve some problem or complete some partially specified task.

Tentativeness heuristic: A perspective to use while engaging the skill of induction; willingness to keep making observations to test the general claim and to alter that claim when observations fail to support the full span of the general claim.

Tolerance for ambiguity: A trait where people are comfortable with a degree of uncertainty when making decisions.

Umbrella sentence: The first sentence in an abstract that communicates to your audience the central essence of the focal object.

Vehicles: The way media messages are delivered; with news messages, the vehicles are the names of different newspapers, news magazines, TV news shows, and news websites.

Vertical thinking: Systematic, logical thinking that proceeds step by step in an orderly progression from problem to solution, typically by following algorithms.

Word budget: The size limit of an abstract typically expressed in number of words, but it can also be expressed as a time limit.